# SOMEWHERE THE DEAD ARE SINGING

# SOMEWHERE THE DEAD ARE SINGING

## Karl Petry

Visionary Living Publishing/Visionary Living, Inc.
New Milford, Connecticut

*Somewhere the Dead Are Singing*

By Karl Petry

Copyright 2021 by Karl Petry

Cover art by Leslie McAllister
Jacket and interior design by Leslie McAllister
Photographs © by Karl Petry unless otherwise noted.

ISBN: 978-1-942157-54-0 (pbk)

Published by Visionary Living Publishing/Visionary Living, Inc.
New Milford, Connecticut
www.visionarylivingpublishing.com

# TABLE OF CONTENTS

*Rosemary Ellen Guiley at an event in New Jersey, 2013. Photo by Karl Petry.*

# A Tribute

I'm fortunate that in my life, I've made friends with so many interesting people. I seem to attract actors, researchers, artists, engineers, filmmakers, psychics, mediums, CIA and FBI personnel, pilots, and authors, to name a few.

Out of them all, the celebrity who most profoundly impacted my life was the famed author, Rosemary Ellen Guiley, to whom this book is dedicated. Rosemary wrote over sixty books, including encyclopedias dealing with the paranormal. In this field she was a leading authority. Her popularity was vast and continued to grow when she became a regular guest on the nationally syndicated Coast-to-Coast AM radio show with George Noory.

Many people benefited from her writings. Hollywood screenwriters used her encyclopedias for accuracy and content in writing for films dealing with paranormal issues.

My relationship with Rosemary began when she visited the Parapsychology Foundation in New York. Rosemary heard of my psychic abilities from Dr. Joanne McMahon and wanted to meet me. The next day I stopped by the Foundation and met Rosemary for the first time. I discussed in detail the abilities I have, and the problems associated with them. I must have made a good impression because after that day we became close friends.

One of the first things I recall that made a lasting impression with her was when she told me she wanted to move from her apartment in Annapolis, Maryland. She still wanted to reside in Maryland and was checking out apartments in various towns. I asked her if there was a town in Maryland named Towson. She said there was, and I said, "You'll find the apartment you want in that town within a few days." Two days later, she called to tell me she found the perfect apartment in Towson.

Mention her name in the paranormal field, and people will always bring up her accomplishments. Yes, she was an expert in this area with a wealth of information and could summon up answers to questions faster than Google, but she was much more than her books, and that was the Rosemary I knew.

Whenever I had an investigation that needed an enthusiastic partner, she was there. From being part of a team to spend the night in a storage facility where a shadow person existed to visiting Ground Zero of the 9/11 World Trade Center tragedy, she was there. When I produced my low budget films and needed a known celebrity for credibility and to spice up the movie, Rosemary always came through, portraying the paranormal expert. She even used her real name in my films!

At the Freemason's club, she was a celebrity and was always friendly and gracious. She never tired of or seemed bothered by the members and guests' attention as they asked for autographs or wanted answers to their ghostly questions. I watched as she gave everyone who approached one hundred percent of her attention, treating them as if they were the only person in the room.

At various conferences, I was with her where occasionally someone would pose the most outlandish question for her to answer. Hearing the same question, I couldn't even understand it, never mind answering, but Rosemary would somehow offer a reply that would satisfy them. She certainly had patience and a commendable attitude.

We would sit in my living room many nights and have lengthy conversations about our upcoming lectures and the subjects we would be discussing. Sometimes we would tap into the latest UFO news our friends from MUFON (Mutual UFO Network) were releasing. When we presented at the same venue, Rosemary had the crowd glued to their seats and hanging on to each word she said. Accompanying her talk was a well-thought-out PowerPoint presentation. She would spend days working on it, and it showed. Of course, when it was time for me to face the same crowd, I was there a cappella, with no PowerPoint, just a sheet with a few keywords to guide me through my talk. Our different styles worked for us.

The last thing I expected was to receive the news that Rosemary was diagnosed with cancer. She began treatments, but all they seemed to do was make her weak and sick. She felt the treatments were more lethal than cancer.

She continued her speaking engagements until the very end. No one knew how dire her health was, and she wanted to keep it that way. On her last visit to my place, as we spoke late into the night, I said to her in passing that she was immortal and would be known for generations to come for her work. She smiled and said I was probably right.

Even at the end of her life, she was a regular television program authority; appearing on the TRVL Channel's *Paranormal Caught on Camera*. The show would present a video of a paranormal scene captured on camera or cellphone, and Rosemary, with a few others, would give their opinions of what it could be. Rosemary stayed with the program until she was physically unable.

The last time Sue and I saw her was Memorial Day weekend, 2019, at her home in Connecticut with her husband, Joe Redmiles. We sat and talked for a few hours, then we all went out for lunch at the local diner. She was very weak but managed to make it through the meal. Before we left to return home, Joe and Rosemary stood in the driveway, waving to us as we departed. I said to Suzy that this is the last time we'll ever see Rosemary, and, sadly, it was.

I will never meet a woman like Rosemary again. She was tops in her field and tops as a friend. There was a part of me that died with her.

The world will miss her, especially the long list of her family and friends. With my highest respect and admiration, I dedicate this book to Rosemary Ellen Guiley.

# A Testimonial

By V. Louise Lang

I have known Karl for the better part of 20 years. In that time, I have seen him use his talents to help many people in need. His calm, reassuring manner and deliberate approach never fail to comfort and reassure people in distress.

Karl has helped me personally, to weather a bleak time in my life. Several years back, I was devastated by the sudden illness and death of a beloved pet. In my darker moments of depression, Karl always found a way to counsel me. His sound advice never failed to lift me out of myself and show me how to face the challenges head on. His guidance came from both his intuitive gifts as well as his practical life experience. Thanks to Karl, I was able to persevere through this dark period and live to be blessed with another wonderful dog that brought me much joy and companionship.

Karl and his wife Suzy, who I dearly love for having put up with me during that horrible time, are truly the best friends anyone could have. And, we all have had many great adventures since then.

I learned that if you open your mind, you will discover the strange and wonderful things that this world holds. And trust me, you will be amazed. But that is for another book from Karl.

# FOREWORD
### By Joseph Redmiles

I met Karl in 2013, through my wife, Rosemary Ellen Guiley. Karl was both a professional colleague and personal friend of hers. They had known each other for many years, had conducted numerous supernatural investigations together, and had lectured at UFO events in the Northeast.

Rosemary often spoke highly of Karl. She praised his psychic abilities and told me how he used his talents to help people through the grief of losing loved ones, to locate missing and treasured possessions and heirlooms, or to reassure those who were going through difficult circumstances that things would work out and to ease their fears. Rosemary always said, "Karl has real talent, he is the real thing."

Rosemary was invited to speak at FRINGE New Jersey, a local UFO organization, in May 2013. I looked forward to attending the event with my wife, because Karl was also scheduled to appear. I was eager to finally meet this person whom I'd heard so much about.

Rosemary introduced us, and Karl and I quickly became friends. We had much in common. We were about the same age, had had similar blue-collar upbringings, and shared many of the same experiences going through school, making our careers, and finding success in life.

We also discovered a shared interest in B-movies, books, and music, along with the paranormal and unexplained. I was tremendously impressed when I found out that Karl had produced and directed several movies. He generously gave me copies and soon I was savoring *The Ironbound Vampire*, *The Haunting of Danbury House*, and *The Larksville Ghost*.

The FRINGE event launched a new phase in Rosemary and Karl's professional association. Over the next couple of years, the three of us conducted several investigations of haunted properties and interviewed more than a few people with fascinating stories of mysterious experiences. You will read of one such investigation in this book. It was during this investigation that I had my breakthrough experience and began to realize the full potential of my own psychic and mediumistic abilities. I must thank Karl for enabling this opportunity.

Karl is a natural-born storyteller. In his new book, *Somewhere the Dead Are Singing,* he weaves the accounts of his psychic experiences with personal anecdotes of his everyday life. The stories are humorous, intriguing, exciting, poignant, and moving. Karl shows how the disparate elements of his life work together to help him maintain a balance and keep his psychic abilities in perspective. He's helped in no small part by his eclectic circle of friends. Actors, producers, fellow psychics, classic car enthusiasts, these are but a few of the kinds of people in Karl's orbit.

In the years since we first met, my friendship with Karl has deepened. We've enjoyed many good times together, comparing notes about our respective childhoods, going to car shows, relaxing in the evenings watching movies from his vast collection. Karl has been a tremendous support to me through Rosemary's final illness and passing. We've helped each other to process our loss.

I'm blessed to call Karl one of my closest friends. As you read the stories contained in his latest book, I am confident that you will come to know him better and to feel a connection with him. I hope that his experiences and stories will resonate with you and cause you to reflect on the events that have made your own life special.

Joseph Redmiles
Memorial Day, 2021

# Cast of Characters

If there is one positive thing about being a psychic, it's the wonderful mix of people you meet. My friends are an assortment of unusual personalities. They include psychics, authors, actors, television and movie personnel, remote viewers, artists, magicians, and paranormal investigators.

A common trait among creative people is that they are, for the most part, non-judgmental of others. Wouldn't you like to be a fly on the wall when we all get together? We discuss a varied range of topics, and none are dull.

At least twice a year, I'm invited to a yard party in Central New Jersey by a woman named Patty. What initially brought her guests together was their belief in the existence of UFOs. There's Pat, a man who retired from the post office. He is considered one of the world's prominent authorities on UFOs. Then there's George Hansen, author and paranormal investigator, and Michael, a former reporter for New Jersey's largest newspaper.

Once, at the party, a group of us were seated in Patty's gazebo, where one of the guests told everyone about his girlfriend from Venus. A few years back, a Philadelphia newspaper carried a story about this man's long-distance love affair. He took a newspaper clipping from his wallet and passed it around the group while telling us the details of his story.

Over by the pool, another woman discussed her abduction by aliens. I won't say it didn't happen, because in truth, maybe it did. The story she told was a captivating account of her nightmarish experience. Earlier, when the public heard of her story, filmmakers from one of the local universities made a film about it. The film was called *Alice,* and a few of the people involved with the event were actors in the movie!

I love these people. To me, they are authentic and genuine. They are unpretentious. Above all, they are fascinating.

I enjoy having people over to my house too. I remember one Thanksgiving when we had a large group of family and friends together. Ingo (the remote viewer) remarked that he remote-viewed different planets. Paula, known as the English Psychic, said she once remote-viewed the moon.

I do not doubt that they both remote-viewed these heavenly bodies; their reputations are well beyond reproach!

However, some of my family members were stunned by hearing those comments, and who could blame them? Like most families, they are accustomed to mundane conversations about the weather, vacations, and, for younger parents, how well their babies are handling bathroom training. I'll always remember that Thanksgiving when my friends stopped this mindless idle chat dead in its tracks. To me, this was the best Thanksgiving ever.

## Vampires and Comics

I was producing a public access show on Manhattan Cablevision called *Vampires*. It was my friends who made the show so successful. I must repeat what I said earlier; they are unique people and certainly not at all boring. Thanks to them, my show's ratings were the highest among all the cable access shows featured. One ratings grabber was Debbie D from Philadelphia, PA. She's also known as Destiny, the Vampire Mermaid, and even a comic book was created in her honor with the same title. Debbie is an attractive woman with an angelic personality.

For years she was chosen as the head mermaid at the annual Coney Island Mermaid Parade.

To make the TV show's episodes interesting, I covered some unusual venues around the New York City area. One unforgettable incident with Debbie D was at the annual New York comic book convention held in New York City. It was held in the basement of a Catholic church, over a weekend, usually in late August. The convention had comic books for sale and featured personal appearances by celebrities of low-budget horror films. Vendors sold their homemade vampire and horror films. Artists specializing in comic book art proudly displayed their paintings and drawings. Many who arrived at the convention, young and old, wore costumes to pay homage to their superheroes or some grisly horror fiends. One vendor was a woman selling copies of her book, in which she told of her experience as a vampire and the difficulties her daughter was going through having vampire blood surging through her veins.

I made sure we interviewed her for the show! But it was Debbie who made the whole trip worthwhile.

As I said before, Debbie is a lovely and angelic person, and she didn't comprehend that we were in the basement of a real church.

She was having some publicity photos taken. The photographer suggested she pose nude using the church as a background.

So, Debbie agreed and followed the photographer from the basement upstairs to the actual church. Debbie took off her clothes and posed in the nude on the altar while the photographer snapped away. Things were going well until the parish priest walked into the church from the sacristy. "What are you doing?" He yelled. "This is sacrilegious!" Debbie spoke up, saying, "Is this a real church?" "Yes, it is!" the priest shouted. She apologized, put her clothes back on, and left the church with the photographer, returning to the basement. That was just half the story because the best was yet to come. Debbie was not the only person at the convention who thought this was not a real church.

It was just past noon, and I was hungry, so I stepped outside to buy a hot dog from one of the food vendors parked on the street. It was a typical August day in New York and was unbearably hot and humid.

I wondered what those food vendors thought as they saw a sea of costumed characters on this hot day buying food, chips, soda, and water, and it wasn't even Hallowe'en.

Walking back to the basement, I noticed a hearse parked in front of the church. I could hear organ music faintly coming from inside the church; the closed doors muffled the sound of the music.

Suddenly, the music got louder as ushers latched the church doors to stay open. I saw well-dressed people filing out of the church, followed by pallbearers carrying a casket. As they approached the stairs, several costumed vampires ran up to the casket and grabbed the side rails next to the pallbearers. They thought they were helping to guide it down the stairs to the sidewalk to the waiting hearse.

The young men in vampire garb, some with exposed fangs, mixing with the legitimate pallbearers, made for quite a sight. A few of the male mourners standing by the church doors started to laugh, but the women, obviously family members, were yelling and screaming at the sight of vampires carrying their deceased family member down the stairs.

The vampires must have thought a movie was being shot, and they wanted to be in it.

At the end of the day, I had my video footage for the television show, and Debbie had new photos she could sell. By the way, that Catholic Church no longer rents out their basement for comic book conventions.

## Roswell

Over the years, I've produced many low budget films ranging from horror and thriller epics to documentaries. One such documentary was called, *Roswell? YES!*

While visiting my friend Ingo Swann at his home in the Bowery of Manhattan, he put on a VHS video showing his friend, Bob Durant, presenting to an audience at a Central New Jersey UFO conference. I watched Bob address the crowd about his twenty-year investigation of the 1947 UFO crash that took place outside of Roswell, New Mexico.

Many believe the United States government has covered up the story about an extraterrestrial spacecraft that crashed there. People who study cases involving Unidentified Flying Objects are known as Ufologists, and this crash is often referred to as The Roswell Incident.

The VHS video Ingo showed me was of poor quality. At the presentation, a camera was set up on a tripod, aimed at the podium then turned on with no operator to control the movement of the camera. When Bob walked out of the camera's view, he just disappeared off the screen.

Despite its production shortcomings, you could see that Bob Durant was an excellent speaker with a powerful and convincing voice.

Ingo told me that Bob was an airline pilot who had just retired and was a firm believer in the existence of Unidentified Flying Objects. After viewing the video, I told Ingo that I was very impressed and would like to professionally produce Bob's presentation using state of the art video equipment, Dolby sound, proper lighting, a narrator, and recorded in a soundproof studio. The result would make for a fabulous documentary.

Ingo thought my idea was excellent and gave me Bob's phone number. Later that evening, I called Bob and told him I saw his taped Roswell presentation and would like to redo it. At first, he sounded overly cautious, probably thinking I was some kind of a scam artist.

But when I told him that Ingo was the one who showed me the video and gave me his phone number, his demeanor changed. He said he thought my idea was a good one, and he agreed to do the project.

During the next few weeks, I followed up with all the details for the shoot. I found a studio in Montclair and arranged for Dr. Joanne D.S. McMahon to be the interviewer. Through Bob's connections, I was able to get original photos of the crash site in New Mexico and would insert those photos during the taping to enhance the program. The images I acquired looked like a typical scene of a desert landscape that could have been taken in any desert, but Bob made sure it was the right location and knew the man who took the photos. The cost wasn't cheap, but I made sure we had them because Bob was a stickler for details.

The interview with Bob took only a day at the studio. Bob was comfortable in front of the camera, and the shoot went flawlessly. The next step was to tape an audience's reaction to what Bob said during the interview.

Although it wasn't shot on the same day, we had to make it seem as if it was. The MC for the audience portion was June Marlowe, an actor I used in my film, *The Ghosts of Angela Webb*. June is a tall, pretty woman with long blonde hair, and her voice at times sounds like Mary Steenburgen.

The following week, we planned to have the audience assemble at the Higgins Center library in Hillsdale, NJ. The audience would be facing a monitor placed in the front of the room with the camera facing the audience. The plan was that the monitor would play Bob's interview, then at certain times, we would stop the interview, and June would ask certain people in the audience their reactions to what Bob said.

The day of the shoot came, and everything was ready for the audience segment. We had the chairs, monitor, lighting, sound equipment, and camera set up; all we needed was an audience to begin shooting. To my horror, people who said they'd be there didn't show up. In short, we had an almost empty room with rows of vacant chairs. I enlisted my father-in-law and mother-in-law, and a few actors I knew to fill the chairs, but the room was still bare. Thinking quickly, my wife made a few calls to her friends who worked for the FBI and the ATF (Bureau of Alcohol, Tobacco, and Firearms), and they came with some of their co-workers. On camera, you could see clean-shaven young men and professionally dressed women sitting in the audience. I then realized that most of the audience was "packing." Yes, weapons strapped to their legs and under their jackets. The shooting was finally over, and in the end, the completed *Roswell? YES!* documentary was successful. It sold at the Roswell Museum, through the Internet, and from ads that I ran in various UFO themed magazines, and of course, eBay. Famed producer Steven Spielberg bought a copy and called to compliment me on an excellent documentary. By the way, I didn't tell him that the audience was "packing."

Being creative is rewarding. Without my intervention, a great program would never have been made, and we'd be left with a poor VHS copy of a fantastic program, which in a short time would have been long lost and forgotten.

By now, you're probably thinking, why did I write about all this? It has nothing to do with having psychic abilities, which is true. I wanted my readers to understand that my life is not living in a world that is entirely based on the paranormal. I believe the fabric of my life is interwoven between a paranormal and a normal existence.

I heeded the warning that Dr. McMahon once said to me, I would be one miserable individual if I dedicated a hundred percent of my life channeling my paranormal abilities.

Things I see from the past are seldom happy, and with those images come emotional empathy, which assures a sad time. Once I'm freed from these images and take on other tasks like working on movies, cars, home repairs and my participation as a Freemason, it puts my mind at rest so when I do take on a paranormal venture, I am truly in the proper state of mind and my psychic accuracy will be heightened.

# The Making of a Psychic

I first met parapsychologist Dr. Joanne McMahon at the Parapsychology Foundation. Over many conversations with her, I shared my personal life history. As our friendship grew, Joanne came to understand the events that had shaped me.

She volunteered that I had the perfect background for being a psychic, but I should always keep one foot in reality.

I knew what she meant.

Many psychics tend to remove themselves from everyday life and enter the paranormal world exclusively. That is something I could never do. When I concentrate on something psychically, I experience a significant amount of mental and physical discomfort. Maybe other psychics don't experience pain, or they grow to accept the discomfort this work generates, but I cannot. A steady diet of psychic concentration would make life miserable for me. That is why I pick and choose my psychic assignments. This formula has worked well for me over the years.

My psychic ability differs from others' in that I can see the past clearly and with a high degree of accuracy. When I tap into an event, I focus on details like the clothing the people wear, the words they speak, the weather, and all the other, minor details of the scene. When I can confirm even the slightest detail of my vision, I'm overjoyed, and that makes me want to push myself to see more and to get the details of the image right.

For example, at a family gathering, I was sitting in the living room with my Uncle Stan directly across from me. An image from his teenage years came pouring into my mind. I quietly told my wife, Sue, to observe what I was about to do, so she could later recall what transpired.

I turned to Uncle Stan and said, "Didn't you work around New Jersey Railroad Avenue when you were a teenager?"

"Yes," he said and added, "It was a tannery."

I went into details that only he would know. "Every day you would have your lunch on New Jersey Railroad Avenue. You sat in a doorway of a three-story building where all you saw in front of you was the stone wall that elevated the railroad."

He acknowledged that, and then I went further. "Every day, you ate a bologna sandwich for lunch and carried it in a paper bag."

Once again, he nodded his head in confirmation.

I glanced at Sue for my last bit of recall. "Didn't a guy from inside the building open the door and ask you to move?"

Uncle Stan replied, in an angry tone, "Yes, he didn't want me to sit in the doorway and told me to sit somewhere else. I told him there was no other place for me to sit. He would just walk away."

Then our conversation hit Uncle Stan, and he said to me, "How old are you?"

I just smiled at him. The fact is that his tannery days were back in the 1930s, decades before I was born. It was these forgotten images that I was tapping into. It wasn't an earth-shaking revelation, just an exercise to keep my mind busy by testing myself. I didn't mention another aspect of this; not only did I see my uncle sitting on that doorway step, but I also felt his loneliness while he sat there without anyone to talk to him. He would stare at the large stone wall in front of him, occasionally glancing up as the trains passed overhead bound for Newark's Penn Station a quarter mile away.

## Reality, Newark Style

In my case, psychic work has never been a source of income. I've always relied on jobs and side work to support myself and my interests. You would think that the older a person got, the fewer opportunities they would have to find work. But I have handy skills in carpentry, painting, electrical, and cement work. Someone always needs something done, so I have a steady stream of calls for my abilities, usually from family and friends.

My many careers broadened my experience and taught me invaluable lessons about humanity. Since I was young, I've always worked, and it rarely mattered what kind of work it was. Some of my early jobs I look back on now with a sense of wonder and amusement.

When I was sixteen, I did occasional work for a plumbing contracting company a few blocks from home.

My friends Vinnie, Anthony, Jimmy Jr., and Michael also worked there. The owner, Jim, looked out for us and would always find work for us. He knew we didn't come from families that showered us with cash, so he found ways to put a few bucks in our pockets. The money we earned gave us some independence and made us all feel good.

One day Jim called and asked my friends and me to be at his house at 8:00 that night. It was summer; we were out of school and glad to have a chance to pick up some spending money.

We showed up at Jim's house at the appointed time, and he issued us each a plastic bucket and a small sledgehammer. Intrigued, we asked, what was the job?

"We're going out to the dump to get some lead," Jim said. "It shouldn't take long."

With that, we all piled into the back of a three-quarter-ton Chevy pickup. We headed to the dump, where Newark disposed of all the broken or cracked cast iron sewer pipes they dug up as they made repairs.

Now, you need to understand how sewer pipes are connected. At the end of one pipe is a collar. Another pipe slides into this collar. To secure the connection, the plumber packs a rope-like material called oakum around the inside of the collar and pours hot lead around it to make a watertight seal. Some of these pipes are huge, over twelve inches in diameter.

Cast iron is strong and can last underground for a hundred years or more. However, it is brittle. One blow on the collar with a sledgehammer causes it to break in pieces.

Once the pipe shatters, the lead is easy to remove.

We arrived at the dump, jumped out of the truck, and headed for the pipes that were lying on the ground.

I was pounding away with my sledgehammer when I heard something inside the pipe. I looked up in time to see a large rat shoot out the far end and scurry off into the bushes.

The pipes were infested!

We kept at the job until we got all the lead and filled almost all the buckets we'd brought. No one got bit, and no rats were injured during this nighttime jaunt.

Jim told us to come back to his place the next night, at the same time. We were to finish the job, melt the lead, and turn the scrap metal into shiny new ingots to use on his future contracting jobs.

I stopped by earlier in the afternoon and saw four propane burners in his yard, the kind used by contractors to melt lead at job sites. Jim had also acquired thick, iron ladles and two tables with ingot forms.

Over dinner that night, I told my father that I was working and would be home late.

"What kind of work?" he asked.

I replied, "We're smelting lead for Jim over at his house."

My friends and I met at Jim's at eight o'clock, ready to get started. Jim fired up the burners, and we began melting the lead.

It was filthy work.

We put the scrap into the ladles, placed them on the burners, and once it melted, an older guy, a friend of Jim's, would slowly pour the molten lead into the forms. As it cooled, we removed the ingots and piled them off to the side for future use.

We finished up around 1:00 a.m., and I went home. When I looked in the mirror, I was surprised to see my face covered in soot. My clothes had a terrible, smoky smell.

I later found out that my father had walked by while we worked to see what was going on. He said that it looked like the fires of Hell! He told my mother that, as he approached the house, all he could see was thick, black smoke above the trees. He said that when he got to the yard, it looked like a factory, with guys dumping lead into ladles, the burners making an orange inferno, and smoke billowing up into the sky. Not something you'd expect to see in your average residential neighborhood.

## Teenage years

I hadn't come to terms with the odd things I saw psychically at this point in my life. It was a quirky thing I managed to keep under wraps.

It never occurred to me to admit I had psychic abilities. My life was complicated enough. I was still in high school and was part of a rock group named Cringe. After school, I had a part-time job at the Federal Pacific Electric Company, delivering mail to their Thornton Street factory. When I wasn't practicing with the group, I tried to find extra work to save money to buy a truck.

I just shook off the psychic images that popped into my head. By not talking about or acting on these images, I believe I became psychically stronger. I had time to process the images without having to explain or make sense of them.

# How Long Have You Had This Ability?

I've been asked many times about my psychic abilities. My answer has always been, I didn't know it was anything special, I thought everyone had it. There is a deeper, more involved answer than my one sentence response. To give you a better perspective, I'll start at the beginning.

It was the early 1960s, I was a young boy living with my family in an apartment on the top floor of a building, in a working-class neighborhood of Newark, New Jersey. It was not a setting conducive to talking about psychic experiences, or anything that might be considered flighty. I wanted to keep a low profile, and never do anything that might draw attention from the adults around me.

Our neighbors were mostly Polish and Italian families. World War II ended little more than a decade earlier and most of the men were veterans. When these men got together, they would reminisce about their days in the war, the places they visited, and the people they met. But I never heard them speak of the horrors of battle. Perhaps they withheld those stories when children were present.

The end of the war brought ships returning home, loaded with thousands of young soldiers, traumatized and suffering from what we now know as PTSD, Post Traumatic Stress Disorder. My father and his brothers all served and were among them. It didn't take much to set them off. One slight infraction by their children or wives usually resulted in a severe scolding or worse, a beating of some kind. In those days, this was a common occurrence. Many of my friends and fellow students had their share of the strap or a backhand from their father. If you wanted to lessen the risk of your father's wrath, you had to be careful of your actions, be mindful of what you said, and do nothing to draw negative attention.

One soldier with an extreme case of PTSD was our neighbor Victor. He was a Pole who had fought with the Russian army. Victor lived on the first floor of our apartment house with his wife, son, and two daughters. He was so quick to anger that the son and older daughter developed a facial tic, from the father constantly slapping them.

I'll never forget one incident with Victor. A man who had been a soldier in the German army moved into the neighborhood. One winter morning Victor looked out his window and saw this German guy waiting at the bus stop on the corner of Pulaski and Oliver Streets. There was a foot of snow on the ground and the temperature was in the 20s. Victor, wearing only a T-shirt and boxer shorts, opened his window and yelled out, "Nazi!". He ran out into the snow-packed street, in bare feet, towards the man, waving his fists and yelling, "Nazi! Nazi!". The German, warmly dressed in a black knee-length winter coat, ran down the street as fast as he could, in fear of this Polish madman.

I later learned that Victor was one of the Russian soldiers who had liberated a concentration camp. Seeing the horrific carnage of a concentration camp firsthand would explain his violent reaction toward the German man.

My father was not as bad as Victor, but he too could be quick to anger and he had a formidable strength. He worked for the Singer Sewing Machine Company on an assembly line. Standing at his workstation, he would attach a few pieces to the sewing machine, then lift it up onto a moving belt where it would travel to the next assembly station. This repetitive action hour after hour gave my father the arm muscles of a prizefighter.

One night, my father was taking our garbage to the trashcans in the yard and I went along with him. As we approached the door to the building, Milton, the landlord's alcoholic son, walked up to my father and demanded some money from him, ending with "Or else!" With ease, my father picked Milton off the ground, pushed him onto the side of the building, cocked his left arm, his most powerful arm, and was about to land a punch when guys from the tavern across the street came running, warning my father to put him down. They knew that one punch from my father could kill Milton, so they called to him, "Walt, put him down, you'll kill him, and you'll go to jail." My father lowered Milton to the ground, and we proceeded back to our apartment. I'm sure my father's PTSD played a large part in this episode.

Living across the street from Johnny's Tavern had its good points. Sometimes, for lunch, my mother would send me there to pick up hamburgers. I would walk through the bar area, climb four steps to the kitchen where the cook mass-produced these lunch time burgers. Every seat at the bar was filled. The men were loud, laughing, smoking cigarettes, and downing beer before returning to work. Can you imagine this happening today?

Johnny's had a television bolted on a shelf in one corner. Thick chains suspended the set from the ceiling. The TV was always on and showed a fuzzy, black-and-white picture with a garbled tone coming from its speaker. Most of the time it was tuned to a Yankee's game.

What impressed me the most, though, as a small lad, was a wire stretched across the bar room. A toy monkey on a bicycle would peddle across the room on this wire. The bartender would activate the monkey by tugging on the wire. Seeing that monkey make his way from wall to wall amazed me and that alone made the trip to get those lunchtime burgers worthwhile.

However, some memories of the bar weren't happy ones. I'll never forget seeing a large, armless man at the bar. He had lost his arms during the war. He would lower his head close to the bar to take sips from a whisky or beer glass. A few times I saw him ask the man next to him to go with him to the bathroom, obviously to help him relieve himself. Seeing this as a young boy disturbed me very much. But that was the time we lived in. Veterans were putting their lives back together, trying to make up for their four-year absence. Normalcy for them began with marriage, starting families and holding down a good steady job. Anything that got in the way of this planned vision of life was asking for trouble.

Which brings us back to the original question. At that time, for a son like me to tell his father and mother that he senses and sees things that others can't, would not be acceptable and would be considered nonsense. Just to raise the subject would have angered my father and would no doubt have resulted in severe disciplinary action. I'm sure he would have feared that if word got out, how would he explain that his son might be crazy and be living his life in Rod Serling's *Twilight Zone*? This was not part of the post-war guide to life and I knew it. If I ever had any thought of discussing my visions with my parents, relatives, or teachers those thoughts were dropped. I spoke to no one about my abilities. I had no idea what I was experiencing and kept anything unusual to myself.

Living like this was stifling. My friends didn't have it much better. There was Anthony and his brother James; the others were Dennis, Vinnie, and Mike. We found refuge in creative outlets. James took a chance at being an actor. He managed to get bit parts and was often in background scenes of films and soap operas. He even did a one-man show in an off-off Broadway play and was very good at it. The rest of us pooled our talents to form a rock band. We called ourselves Cringe.

We were novice musicians but overall, we were surprisingly good. Most of our songs were originals and we spent hours practicing.

The songs were a joint effort by the band members. The subjects of our songs were varied and unusual. One song, *Concrete Forest*, was a mournful dirge about how we felt being young and living in the big city. The lyrics were both sad and powerful and had a creepy side.

We never knew how the public was going to accept our band and our songs. We were still in high school and our band was unknown.

My brother Mark was attending St. Peter's College in Jersey City at the time and when he heard that some of the students were throwing a party in Staten Island, NY, he got us to play for it. We thought *Concrete Forest* would be a good song to start our set.

The party was held in the basement of a huge home. It had all the trappings of a New York style nightclub with a huge bar and mirrored walls. Once we finished setting up, I introduced the band. The crowd ignored me and carried on with their socializing.

The first notes of *Concrete Forest* start with the sound of funeral bells. Our inspiration was one Saturday when Anthony, the guitar player, and I passed St. Casmir's Church while a funeral was taking place. We heard from one of our friends standing on the sidewalk that it was for a young man who died. The bells played two mournful notes over and over the entire time the pallbearers loaded the casket into the hearse. We duplicated that bell sound and started the song with it.

Now, here we were in front of a group of college students who probably expected us to blast one of the top ten hits. Instead, we began with the sound of funeral bells. I was the singer and after the first few verses everyone stopped talking and was staring at us. Halfway through the song I became very nervous, no one was moving, they were just looking at us. At the end of the song, we were expecting at least a few people to applaud but we didn't get even one. I glanced at my brother to get his reaction and I'm sure he was as shocked as I was.

We were getting ready to start the second song when one of the students walked up to me and said, "Wow, that was cool." He was a writer for the St. Peter's College newspaper and wanted to know everything about the song. He asked for a copy of the lyrics. The next issue of the college paper featured a story about "the high school group with original and dynamic music," along with the lyrics of *Concrete Forest*. We felt encouraged that our hard work and many hours of practice had paid off.

I joined a work-study program while I was in my junior year in high school. I spent four hours in school, in the morning. In the afternoon I worked at an electrical manufacturing company, where I delivered mail to the offices and the factory. I got on well with everyone who worked there including many of the executives. My work relationships soon opened doors for our band. I was asked to perform at their private parties. It made them feel cool to hire an inner-city rock group for entertainment.

These private parties were usually held at an executive's palatial home. Some of them went on for two days and were wild, where anything goes. Starting with smoking weed and escalating to bed hopping by the guests. We just played our music and stayed out of the way. Mike, our drummer, accidentally walked into a bedroom where all the women were lying on the bed with little or no clothes on. About an hour later, these women returned to the living room, where we were playing. Then we noticed all the men suddenly disappeared.

I must say that the boys in the band were tight lipped and nothing we saw at those parties ever left the building. Our hosts treated us like kings. They provided all the meals and whatever drinks we wanted. When we returned to school on Monday, we made sure not to tell anyone where we'd been over the weekend.

Some of my classmates were pushing for our band to play at the school dances. I always found a reason why we couldn't: we didn't want to ruin a good thing.

I read an ad in the New Jersey *Star Ledger* about talent scouts looking for bands with original music. I answered the ad, and we scheduled an audition for 2 PM on a Sunday at a home in Union, a town a few miles from us. We started with *Concrete Forest*, and when the song finished one of the men asked if we had any more songs like that. We did and performed two more songs. When we finished, they asked who wrote the songs. I answered that I wrote them with Dennis. They wanted to talk to us in private, so the two of us went with them to the kitchen. They said they were looking for songwriters for Gary Lewis and the Playboys, a popular band in the 1960s. They really liked our songs and style and said they'd be calling me the next day.

They called and offered me a job to write songs for Gary Lewis. However, I would have to relocate to California. Being only sixteen, my parents turned down the job. Although it was an opportunity lost, I was pleased that the scouts had considered us talented enough to make an offer.

Those song lyrics came from within me. It was the way I looked at life. Now reflecting on those times, I realize that I was writing from the point of view of a person who had a non-conventional way of thinking; someone who had a unique view of life. In retrospect, I was writing from a point of view of a young psychic.

The band didn't last. Life got in the way. Schooling, jobs and relationships took over. If circumstances were different, and we had had financial and moral support, I believe we would have achieved great success in the music business.

I couldn't end this chapter without sharing the lyrics of *Concrete Forest*.

### CONCRETE FOREST[1]

From the shadows of my deepest dreams,
Into the streets I'm hurled,
Where reality is dead it seems,
I'm in an electrical world,
Where the silence are no more,
Where love has met defeat,
I look above to see the roar,
In the Forest of Concrete
(Chorus)
Purple shadows fall all around,
They never touch the ground,
They only touch the trees of the
Concrete Forest

---

[1] Lyrics by Karl Petry. Copyright 1969. Used by permission.

Peppermint Candy fades into night,
In a fifth dimensional land,
Still with the coming of the light,
I don't know where I am,
Just trees of the eerie color of hate
In a kaleidoscopic display,
Tell my mind it's late,
In the darkness of the day
(Chorus)
Soon the dawn will come and I
Shall awaken from, the shackles, bonds,
Concrete Forest, it never comes, it'll never end.

# Cape May, New Jersey

Cape May is a beautiful seashore resort town located at the southernmost tip of New Jersey. If you enjoy Victorian architecture, you'll find a wide assortment of large Victorian homes in the historic district near the shoreline. The Jersey Shore is known for its amusement boardwalks at Seaside Heights, Wildwood and Asbury Park, but Cape May is much quieter, which is what appealed to Sue and me. We live active lives and getting away for a few days is a mini vacation.

It was over twenty years ago when Sue and I decided to take some time off and visit the Cape we heard so much about. We booked our stay at a popular bed and breakfast a few blocks from the ocean. The building was a restored Victorian home with a large porch that wrapped around the building. As an added Victorian touch, the front entrance sported both a British and an American flag overlooking its staircase.

The beach was clean and immense, yet I didn't plan to spend time lying there taking in the sun's rays. My fair skin makes me a candidate for nighttime beach walking and wearing long pants and double-digit sun blocker during the day.

After putting our luggage in our room, we took a walk on the boardwalk. As innocent as this sounds, shortly after our walk began, I experienced a serious problem.

After years of interviews and testing, it was determined that I had the ability known as retrocognition. The term was first used by Frederick W. H. Myers, the founder of the Society for Psychical Research. Wikipedia defines the term as "knowledge of a past event which could not have been learned or inferred by normal means."

Images of Cape May from the past were coming through, and there was no way I could stop them. In my mind, the reality of that day was interrupted by visions dating back over a hundred years. The buildings lining the boardwalk were morphing into structures from the past. Present day people walking on the boardwalk interposed with people from over a hundred years ago.

This blending of time put my senses into a virtual tailspin. I felt like my mind was being torn apart, with a part of me in the here and now, and another part on the boardwalk in the early 1900s. Accompanying the images were smells: a woman's perfume, that of a male passerby, the ocean's salty air, and the odor of horse manure.

As we continued our stroll, the images shifted from the past to the present. About two blocks from where we started, we came to a group of stores. I pointed to one and said to Sue, "That store was a photography studio, with a banner advertising that photographs were taken here." A few fancy horse-drawn carriages with signs designating the hotels would in passing block my vision of the photography studio. In those carriages were travelers making their way down the boardwalk toward their hotels.

On the beach, people mingled, but I can't recall seeing anyone in the water. I saw a young man standing by himself in between a few of the stores. He looked to be about fifteen years old, and he wore a dark suit and a cap. Not something we would consider wearing at a beach resort today. I got a psychic impression that he was a poor boy, and it took everything he had to make the trip here. I felt his immediate concern was how would he make it home without a dime in his pocket, and where would he sleep at night? The boy's shoes were old and battered, which seemed to validate my impression of the lad. As we passed, I glanced at him, and it seemed he looked back at me. What was he seeing? Me, from the twenty-first century? Or possibly someone dressed in late eighteenth-century garb? There is always the possibility that during these episodes I am invisible, unseen by those from the past, and in this case, the boy just happened to look in my direction. I guess I'll never know.

These images came to me at a cost. I was feeling nauseated, something I always experience during my retrocognition visions. With my stomach in a knot, we skipped lunch and walked around the historic district of Cape May. We came upon an antique shop, rather small and with narrow aisles. I was looking over the glassware on the countertop when Sue called to me. She pointed at a large, framed photograph on the wall. Taken in the early part of the twentieth century, it showed the store I pointed to just a short while ago on the boardwalk. A large banner that said "PHOTOGRAPHS TAKEN HERE" hung on the entire length of the storefront. To the right was the blurry image of a horse drawn hotel carriage filled with well-dressed passengers about to pass by. This photo of a moment frozen in time was something I accurately witnessed just a few minutes earlier, over a hundred years later.

Sue never knew when my retrocognition would kick in, but she always knew when it did and never interfered. Something I have no control over triggers images and it's not confined to any schedule, day or night.

On the first day of our stay Sue and I relaxed on the B&B's second floor balcony looking down Ocean Street and facing the ocean. It was late in the afternoon, and a horse-drawn carriage with the driver wearing a top hat came into view. I surmised he was taking visitors on a sightseeing trip, telling them the histories of various houses they passed.

As the carriage turned the corner and the sound of the horses' hooves faded, I resumed my focus on Ocean Street and the ocean in the distance. The colorful sight of the homes, trees and sky turned quickly to shades of gray. What I now viewed was not the hot July day but a cold day in winter.

The setting was night. Snow was falling and drifts were everywhere. Virgin snow lacked any tracks by man or animal on the street or sidewalk. It was quiet; a soft wind was the only sound that accompanied what I was seeing. What year was this? Where were the people? I told Sue what I was experiencing, which after so many years wasn't a surprise. Maybe if I had some sleep, things would return to normal, and we could resume our stay without the drama of bygone era flashbacks.

When I woke up the following morning, the images had returned to normal and the vision of the snowy night had disappeared. We dined at a local restaurant and shopped at the Washington Street Mall, where we purchased a painting of a black cat, which now hangs in our guest room. We finished the night by taking in a show at the Cape May Stage. It was a perfect night, and we still had a few more days to go.

The following night, like the night before, went well, but on the third night I couldn't get any sleep. Images of the snowy night returned, and this time I found myself in a dream state walking down Ocean Street and turning right onto Beach Avenue, which runs along the ocean. Someone had shoveled the snow off the sidewalk, and I could see a few automobiles covered with snow. Now I knew we were either in the mid-to-late 40s or early 50s.

I heard the sound of a truck and saw a flatbed with chains on the rear wheels. The truck passed me. I won't forget the sound of those chains as they chopped their way through the snow or the engine's low rumble that is typical of a low compression flathead engine. I'm familiar with this type of engine since one of my interests is working on old cars. There is a distinct smell of exhaust and burning oil associated with those vintage engines, and the truck that just passed me had its share.

I found a tavern and walked in. The bartender wore a white apron, and two patrons sitting at the bar had on thick coats and hats. The bartender looked at me and for some unknown reason his stare made me feel uncomfortable. I was aware that I was not a part of this time, and even to sit down to have a drink was out of the question. How would I pay for it? My money would be considered counterfeit if it was 1946 and I was paying for my drink with a dollar from the year 2000 or coins from 1980. I turned and walked out, retracing my way back to Ocean Street.

The images of my dream state ended there, and it was time for me to return to the present. Dipping into the past didn't reoccur for the remainder of my stay. What happened on my initial visit to this seashore resort is now all a part of my mind's museum of recollections.

Flip-flopping through time is both interesting and terrifying. When people hear of this ability, they say how wonderful it would be to be able to visit a time in the past, but I assure them that it is not. A television producer, upon hearing of my ability, wanted to make a show based on my retrocognition. His idea was for me to visit places around the world and record what I could see, that no one else could. After meeting with the producer and his people a few times, it was clear I scared them, and the whole idea was shelved. This was not the first time this has happened to me and won't be the last.

Many years have passed since the first time I went to Cape May. Now, I try to visit Cape May at least once during the summer. Visions from the past will always surface during my stay there. I've come to expect them and rarely mention these visions to Sue or anyone else. My biggest fear is that maybe one time when I'm visiting the past during a retrocognition episode, I won't return. Instead, I will exchange this life with another life in a long-forgotten time in the past.

# House for Sale

It was mid-September, and I was visiting my friend Margaret, an independent makeup artist who worked primarily in New York City on television shows and corporate videos. She was complaining to me about having to chase down her money after she does her work. "Why don't they just send me a check like everyone else?" She went on, "I could be sitting on my ass enjoying my free time instead of begging for money due me." There was no hiding it, she was mad, so when she asked if I wanted to take a trip with her to the producer's home to get her money, I agreed. I thought if she exploded at the producer, I could calm her down, keeping her out of trouble.

The producer and her husband lived about ten miles northwest of Nanuet, New York. The trip would take about forty-five minutes, and we planned to stop for lunch on the way back. Once we got off the major highway, we weaved our way down a two-lane macadam road passing through a few picturesque towns. We pulled into a tree-lined driveway facing a newly built, modern style, two-story home surrounded by beautiful landscaping.

Once the car came to a stop, a well-dressed, attractive blonde woman came out of the house and stood on her second-story deck. Margaret said to me, "That's Jennifer." We said our hellos, and Margaret introduced me. Jennifer invited us in for coffee and pastries.

We entered the house from the deck. Margaret and Jennifer soon were busy talking about the shoot they had just finished, a training video for a pharmaceutical company.

I sat at the kitchen island, sipping my coffee and staring at Jennifer. Images of her entered my mind. They morphed into a full-blown visual, like a television program of an incident that happened to her many years ago. After half an hour passed, Jennifer pulled out her checkbook, wrote a check, and handed it to Margaret.

With my coffee gone, along with the apple-filled pastry safely tucked away in my stomach, I knew we were about to leave. I thought to myself, what the hell, I'll never see this woman again, so I'll share my vision to find out if I'm right. If I happen to be wrong, the worst outcome will be that Jennifer will think Margaret has some nutty friends.

Margaret and I walked down the deck's stairs, and when we got to the last step, I turned to face Jennifer. "Were you ever abducted, possibly by a UFO?"

Margaret looked at me as if I had two heads, but Jennifer answered, "Why are you asking me that?"

I told her about the images I saw while I was having my coffee, witnessing what happened to her many years ago. "It occurred at a lake. You were with two other women. It appeared you were on a camping trip. The sun was setting, so you built a campfire, and you saw a bright light moving slowly over the lake. That was the last thing you remembered. Then in what seemed like seconds, you were back at the campsite. The two women were sleeping, the campfire had burned itself out, and you couldn't account for the missing time."

"All that is true," Jennifer said. "The next morning, the women said they had turned around, and I disappeared. They thought I went for a walk."

"You never spoke about it again. You surmised that the strange light you saw came from a UFO that must have abducted you."

Jennifer stood there motionless, then said, "I never told anyone about that, not even my husband. How did you know?"

I answered, "I could see it."

Rather than keep her in a state of confusion, I told her that I could see things like that, and such visions were a common occurrence for me.

Margaret never knew about my having psychic abilities and didn't say much during our ride home. Knowing her down-to-earth personality, where everything is black or white, up or down, she probably was convinced I was a loon.

What I didn't know at the time was that meeting Jennifer would be the start of a lasting friendship, and that we would be collaborating on paranormal investigations for all these many years.

It wasn't long before I got a phone call from Jennifer. She wanted to discuss her abduction in greater detail. A week later, I was on my way to her place, remembering the route taken by Margaret.

We sat in her living room with her monster-sized dog, "Bruno," who kept an eye on us both. During the visit, I did not reveal what I was feeling concerning her house and property. I did not know how she would react, and I needed that information before I would discuss disturbing news with anyone.

I felt an oddness about her property the second I arrived. I felt that someone or something was watching me, either from the woods around the house or from the sky above. I kept all this to myself. The mystery of the place would show itself later, but this was just a beginning. Over multiple cups of coffee, we discussed various paranormal subjects and the many cases I investigated. A few hours later, I bid my good-bye and left.

Jennifer was very active in her work, producing short programs and commercials for television. She started her career as a reporter for a large newspaper. At that time, she was one of the few women reporters working in a man's world, and hiring her was a groundbreaking move by such a large newspaper. She was good at it and won awards for her work. It wasn't long before she parlayed those awards into the more lucrative career she had now.

Every so often, I would stop by to see her, and every time the odd feeling about her place remained. There were signs that didn't escape me. For example, a small tree in back of her house was growing in a strange, twisting fashion. I also noticed that all the trees in the back rarely, if ever, moved with the wind. While other trees nearby swayed in the wind, those on her property did not. Furthermore, that part of New York State is full of wildlife, yet I never saw so much as a deer or squirrel in the yard.

As our friendship grew, so did her psychic ability. "I'm more aware of things around me since I met you," she said. She developed a sixth sense about things in the workplace as well as with family matters. I told Jennifer that when it came to family, I knew from personal experience that showing psychic ability makes one a *persona non grata*. The more accurate you are, the more uncomfortable people around you become, and they soon will dislike you. On the other side of the equation, though, I now had a good friend with growing psychic abilities.

Jennifer kept busy with her work, and we would see each other at various times when our schedules would permit. Sadly, about a year after we first met, her dog, Bruno, passed away, and she brought another puppy, a Giant German Shepherd, into the house. One look at the dog's paws, and you could imagine how large this puppy would become. Right before my eyes, it went from a cute puppy to the size of a Shetland pony. She named him "Mack." He was a gentle soul, but I wouldn't want to get him angry.

Jennifer told me about a strange occurrence that troubled her. She had a light fixture mounted under the deck next to the sliding doors of the lower level. Someone, or something, ripped the fixture off the wall, and the remnants of electrical wires held what was left to sway in the breeze. That night, she and her husband heard the ungodly sound of an animal, but it was like nothing they heard before. Mack was noticeably restless that night, running from the second to the lower level. Jennifer thought maybe he needed to be taken out, so to avoid a major doggie mishap, she put a leash on him and exited the garage onto the driveway. He eventually relieved himself, but all the while, he kept tugging on the leash, looking toward the hill behind the house, then reversed directions south of the house to the base of the hill toward the marshy ground.

Jennifer called me the next day, so I stopped by to see if I could get a handle on what happened the night before. We walked the grounds, and to our surprise, under the deck, we found huge footprints in the soft ground. Bigfoot? I couldn't believe it. I was never a believer in the Bigfoot legends, and now one had landed in my lap. Every fiber in my bones said to look for some other explanation. Just by mentioning "Bigfoot" as the cause of this event, I risked my credibility as a respected psychic. Neither did I want to scare Jennifer. So, I said, "Maybe a bear?" We went back into the house and tried to come up with some other explanation.

Jennifer's husband, Henry, is an accountant who owns a successful firm. Rosemary Ellen Guiley once told me that the worst skeptics are accountants when dealing with the supernatural or paranormal. Their whole world is putting numbers and words in boxes and on lines. If something comes up that can't be put in a box or on a line, to them, it doesn't exist.

The same goes with mathematicians: one plus one is two. The world is based on mathematics, and therefore, everything must add up. When Jennifer's husband refused to believe any of what she and I discussed, it came as no surprise. He had a simplistic answer for every question asked, no matter how lame. "It was a bear!" he insisted when told of the enormous footprint and wouldn't talk about it anymore.

But things were about to change. Jennifer told me sounds frequently echoed through the woods and that Mack's reactions to sounds around the house kept him alert during the night. It was a Thursday, late in the afternoon, almost sundown, when Mack barked and ran to the front door, poised as if to attack.

Jennifer and Henry ran to the back sliding doors to see what was happening outside. Facing them on the hill stood a large, hairy creature, at least eight feet tall. They both froze. Something that massive could easily knock down the front door, Jennifer thought. She got up the nerve to ask Henry, "Is that a bear?"

The creature then turned and retreated into the woods. Despite what he just saw, Henry refused to say it was a Bigfoot. He refused to say anything at all about it.

The following day, I stopped by to see where this all took place. I had said it before, and I would repeat it, there was something weird about this house and its property. Once again, I felt as if I was being watched from the wooded area below the house. After inspecting the grounds, I decided to go to the third floor, where the bedrooms are, to get a view from those windows. When I stepped onto the third-floor landing, I fell to my knees. I had the sensation that the room began to spin violently, making it impossible for me to stand. I crawled down the stairway to the second level, where I was able to compose myself. After that, I could not enter the third floor of that house.

The next day Jennifer walked Mack without his leash in the backyard. The air got very still and quiet, and Mack ran up the hill. Jennifer kept calling him to return, but that eerie silence surrounded her. She was convinced Mack had run off to attack the creature and would certainly be killed. She stood in the woods calling Mack, but the sound of her voice didn't carry and seemed to end abruptly as soon as the words came out of her mouth. Worry soon turned to terror when Mack still didn't return—no sound of his running over the leaves, no barking, nothing. Suddenly, Mack was by her side. How he got there without making a sound is a mystery. Jennifer vowed to walk him on a leash from then on.

I decided to bring a compass and walk the property. It read correctly— north was north and south was south—until I reached the area where they saw the creature. The compass's needle turned to where north was now east, and, after taking a few more steps, north was west. I retraced my steps on another day, and those areas reverted to read correctly; north was north, and so on.

My psychic ability was being tested like never before. Psychically, I felt as if I were straddling two different dimensions. The weird feeling I had when I first stepped onto the property remains to this day. The Bigfoot connection is only a part of the equation. Focusing on other aspects of the surroundings I noticed the absence of wind and wildlife to the south. East of the house, an area that I call "The Zone of Silence," where ambient sounds seem to disappear, I had the feeling I was always being watched from the woods or the sky. And, let's not forget the close encounter with the Bigfoot, which was north of the building, the same area where the compass gave false readings.

In the house, I felt that something was scanning me, that the walls did not shield me from the scrutiny of an outside force. I felt as if an external presence monitored all conversations and thoughts taking place inside the house. I found little difference between visiting a haunted house and this house: both have an unworldly energy.

Jennifer needed to make a decision. Should she try to fix the problems or sell the house? These strange happenings were taking a toll on her and her family. I felt it was time to bring in the big guns. Maybe there was something we were missing. Who better to contact than Rosemary Ellen Guiley and her husband, Joe Redmiles? I called her, and as I expected, she said she would investigate. Dean and Stuart James-Foy, the famed psychic/mediums from England, were visiting Rosemary and Joe and would join the investigative team for added clout.

On a Tuesday night, Rosemary, Joe, Dean, and Stuart arrived at our home. Sue and I were happy to see everyone and we chose the Colonial Diner in Lyndhurst for dinner. Wanting a fresh approach to the investigation, Sue and I were careful not to divulge information about Jennifer's home. Instead, we discussed other subjects, such as Dean and Stuart's fondness for American diners with their supersized portions and variety of foods. The Colonial's artwork was a big hit, featuring a wall mural of 1950s hot rods, uniquely American.

The next morning, we arrived at Jennifer's house. As we pulled in, Jennifer greeted us in the driveway. Always looking her best, she made an excellent impression. She led us into the house where she had refreshments waiting.

Rosemary remained on the two-story deck, pulling out her camera and taking photos of the woods behind the house. I, too, lagged behind and asked her what she was photographing. She pointed to a grouping of downed tree branches and said, "See how the branches make an X? That is a sign that Bigfoot makes to mark territory."

When Rosemary told Jennifer about the Bigfoot territorial X's in the woods, Jennifer felt it was time to tell everyone about her problem with the creatures. Dean and Stuart asked to walk around the house to get a feel for the place. Jennifer gave them a tour, starting on the lower level. I stood away from them so as not to interfere with their impressions. They both were quiet, only occasionally asking a few questions about the rooms. I'll never forget Stuart's fearful expression when he looked through the sliding glass doors that exited into the back of the house. "There is a huge creature that looks into those doors at night," he said.

As Jennifer continued the tour, they were ready to view the third level. Not knowing how the third level had affected me because I had been careful not to divulge anything that might taint their impressions, Dean flatly refused to enter the third floor because of the unsettling feelings he was experiencing. Stuart, however, ventured on.

Joe stayed with Rosemary as she circled the outside of the house. I could see them conversing with one another and Rosemary looking very engaged with her findings.

Rosemary told Jennifer that she would forward the pictures to a Bigfoot expert she knew on the west coast. She was convinced Jennifer was the target of a single, or many, Bigfoot creatures on her property.

Dean and Stuart believed the troubles surrounding the place were genuine and that the opinions and conclusions I derived, based on my many visits, had merit.

We said our good-byes and thanked Jennifer for being such a wonderful hostess. She later told me we all made a good impression.

It has been almost two years since our visit. In that time, Jennifer's neighbors to the north installed a powerful light on the side of their building, so bright it could be seen through the woods and reflect off Jennifer's windows. Shortly after that, the light fixture was torn off and left with only its wires dangling. Those neighbors vacated overnight and put their house up for sale.

The family living across the road removed all trees and bushes in front of their home and installed a massive amount of lighting, making their home glow.

Henry, Jennifer's skeptical husband, one night heard the ungodly screams followed by the horrible odor associated with a Bigfoot and ran out of the house with a loaded shotgun ready to confront the creature. Henry is now a believer.

Jennifer decided to sell her house. Living in this Bigfoot-plagued estate was troublesome. Afraid to walk the dog at night, listening to strange sounds surrounding the house, and having a weapon loaded for a possible supernatural attack was more than she and Henry could handle. Once when I came to see the latest Bigfoot print in the mud, I raised my head and looked toward the house about 400 feet away and thought, this is what the creature sees. During the day and into the early evening, Bigfoot watches the family, then disappears late in the evening or the early morning. Whether this creature is flesh and bone or an inter-dimensional being, I agreed with Jennifer that she should sell the house.

Like their neighbor, Jennifer and Henry didn't need to reveal the real reason for selling; prospective buyers and the real estate people wouldn't have believed them, anyway. They would only question their sanity. It was time for Jennifer and Henry to live in peace, and now they do.

# VISITING THE DEAD

When I get up in the morning, I make my way to the bathroom to obey nature's call, put on my contact lenses, shave, then shower. About then, I'm somewhat awake to check any emails that came in overnight. Don't get me wrong; I'm not fully awake. I'm a night person, and my brain doesn't get into gear till about 10 AM.

When I do sleep, it's very deep sleep. While in this relaxed, deep sleep state, I often experience paranormal visions. The visions are much different than your common dream. It's as if I'm watching a television program where the images are before me, and I have a front-row seat watching and listening. It's an easy time for me to reach those who have passed because there is no physical effort at all. In a sleep state, communication takes little to no effort on both our parts.

As described in his biography, psychic Edgar Cayce, the most documented psychic of all time, would go into a self-induced sleep state. He said his subconscious mind would leave his body and retrieve knowledge from the spirit realm. That would include diagnosing illnesses and suggested remedies. A biographer nicknamed him "The Sleeping Prophet."

Contacting the dead is something I rarely do. Those who have passed usually contact me. Sadly, when I have tried to reach someone close to me who has crossed over, I fail to connect. Other times, someone passes, and that very evening, our spirits are together. After all these years, and with the many experiences I've had, I still have not found a sure-fire formula to contact the dead at will. It is, at best, a hit or miss episode.

On a particular Monday morning, I received an email from Mrs. J, the wife of a man I knew, a Freemason. In her email, she told me about their son, who passed away two weeks previously. She had heard about me and wanted to know if I could stop by their home to see if I could contact her son. The child's death came suddenly, and she had some unresolved issues to discuss with him.

Here I was, confronted with grieving parents wanting me to help them communicate with their son. I didn't answer the email right away because I wanted to think about this request for a while. If I didn't accommodate them, I was sure they would seek out someone else, and for a hefty price, that person would tell them anything they'd like to hear for as long as their money allowed.

However, if I met with these people, there was always a chance I would see or hear something that would put their minds at rest. Since I don't charge for this service, they would have nothing to lose.

I decided to meet with them and to ask Christine Hague to come with me. Whenever possible, I bring Christine to an investigation. I can't remember all the things I say while exploring a site, and Christine is good at remembering the tiniest details and taking notes.

Mrs. J's email included her telephone number, so I called, gave her my condolences, and agreed to meet with them. I made sure I told them in no uncertain terms that I didn't guarantee anything. Mrs. J said she understood. The couple's home was in Bloomfield, just a few towns over from me in Essex County. Christine lived in Belleville, which borders Bloomfield. I called Christine and told her about my new assignment. She agreed to join me. I knew she would because she likes our missions. We decided to meet the J's at their home on a Thursday at 7:30 PM.

That Thursday morning, I had a job videotaping a legal deposition for a court case dealing with medical malpractice. At the time, my full-time job was working as a forensic videographer and photographer. This deposition lasted for four hours. Even though I was mentally exhausted, I still managed to shake it off and was ready to meet the couple in Bloomfield. One thing I insist on is that I don't want to know anything about the deceased. No checking Internet sites or talking to others who knew him or his family. I always like to go in fresh because the information I get from other sources could be wrong, which would confuse my train of thought if I psychically saw something different.

That Thursday night, I drove to Christine's place. I didn't eat because when I concentrate psychically, it puts me under stress. If I eat, I feel nauseous. Christine didn't say much during our short trip, but there wasn't much to say under the circumstances. She has children, and knowing we would be discussing the loss of a couple's son would make any mother feel squeamish.

The J's home was just off Bloomfield's main street. The street lighting wasn't the best, though, and finding house numbers wasn't easy. On the second pass down the street, we found the home and pulled into the driveway. I had tuned my radio to a 1960s station, and we heard the last note of the Beatles song "I Will" before I turned off the engine and we exited the truck.

I rang the doorbell, and Mrs. J answered. We took a few steps into the living room and saw Mr. J seated on the couch. As soon as he saw us, he stood and greeted us with a smile. We all knew why we were there, yet the situation seemed awkward. I introduced Christine, and she sat on a chair to my left. She was nervous, leaning forward with her legs crossed. The couple offered us a drink and some snacks, but Christine and I declined, knowing what I was about to do.

I asked for a photo of their boy, and Mrs. J handed me a framed, eight-by-ten picture. I looked at it for a minute, and then the room's ambient sound got lower and lower. I returned the photo to Mrs. J and waited. It seemed like only another minute before my perception of the room became cloudy. To my right, I had a vision of a road and a boy walking down it. Next to the road was a tree stump. The boy walked to the stump and sat on it. I saw a smoky film come over the living room. Through this cloudy fog, Mrs. J faced me from where she sat at the far end of the room.

Suddenly, entering the room from the left, through the fog-like haze, was an older woman. Once she walked in, I had little or no control over what happened. I became a living telegraph. She spoke, and I repeated her words to the room.

"How is the boy?" I burst out.

"He's fine," she replied. "You don't have to worry about him." She had the biggest smile on her face; it was as if she were waiting for me to show up so she could talk to the J's again.

I turned my head, looked at Mrs. J, and repeated the old woman's question, "How did you like the silver bracelet I left you?"

Mrs. J looked at Mr. J and said, "It's your mother."

"Why don't you bring it out?" said the old woman.

Mrs. J left the room and returned with a silver bracelet.

"That's not it," the woman said.

Mrs. J left and brought out another silver bracelet.

"That's not it," came the answer again.

Mrs. J scooped up the bracelets, left the room, and returned with still another silver bracelet in seconds.

"That's it!" said the woman.

Mrs. J said, "I love this bracelet and wear it all the time."

The old woman gave her a huge smile. "I bought it at Lipton's, my favorite store."

"Lipton's was her favorite store," Mr. J said. "She bought just about everything there."

I later learned that the Lipton department store was in Bloomfield Center, where all the town's main streets intersected, and that store closed many, many years ago.

Mr. J's mother went on to say how much she missed and loved everyone and was happy that Mrs. J was enjoying her jewelry.

I relayed this conversation for quite a few minutes and included many intimate details of the family that only the J's would understand. Christine told me later that it was as if Mr. J's mother sat in the room with us. There was no sign of fright from anyone, but rather a welcoming of her presence. Words flowed from my lips as fast as I could repeat them. It was almost like I was competing in a speaking marathon.

Soon, the conversation's pace got slower, however, and I could tell this visitation was coming to a close. The images I saw were less pronounced, and the voice of Mr. J's mother began to fade. Seconds later, I was back, the vision was gone, and the room's sound returned to normal. Everyone was looking at me, sensing that I had returned from my transcendental trip.

If we learned anything from all this, it was that in the short time we interacted with the other side, we received plenty of information that satisfied Mr. and Mrs. J. We lessened the heartbreak of the boy's passing by hearing that he wasn't left abandoned in the afterlife. I'm sure it was comforting to the J's to know their son had a loving family member to help him during his life/death transition.

Christine and I believe Mr. and Mrs. J were happy with the information I brought to them. I saw no indication that Mr. J's mother wanted me to return so she could continue her conversation with her son and daughter-in-law.

We gave our final goodbyes to Mr. and Mrs. J and drove off to Christine's house. Neither of us said much during this short drive. I was tired, and Christine was still taking in all that she just witnessed. What happened that Thursday night will forever be in our memories. For my part, I felt that I had made a couple in mourning happier. I gave Christine a front-row seat to peek into an undiscovered world, and I thought that I accomplished something virtuous.

The story I just told of Mr. and Mrs. J had a positive, heart-warming conclusion. Not all incidents in dealing with the dead turn out that way. Sometimes, a chain of events can lead you down the rabbit hole to a place you never figured you should be.

One such unforgettable venture with the dead began on a hot day in July. It involved a dried-out piece of newspaper and just plain curiosity on my part. It all started when I was driving down Kossuth Street in my old neighborhood and saw my friend Tony Branco in front of the house where he rented an apartment. A group of men, including Tony, were filling a refuse container with debris from the house's interior. They'd been tearing the old plaster and lathe walls down to the frame because the building's owner planned to rebuild the house with new wiring, plumbing, sheetrock, floors, roofing, and lighting, which would make this old house as good as new. The increased value of the property would more than cover the cost of the renovation.

What I found interesting was that the house was built in 1904. How did I know it was 1904? Back then, it was common for builders to use newspapers as insulation in the walls. Extremely dry pieces of the *Newark Daily Advertiser* were in and around the building. The paper was so brittle that just touching it with any pressure would turn it into dust. By my feet, I saw part of a newspaper's front page dated December 13, 1904, LAST EDITION Two Cents. A headline read, *KEARNY MAN FOUND LIFELESS IN HOTEL*, and under that in smaller font, *Andrew C. Kimball killed by Gas in a Local Hostelry.* Under that headline, in a larger font, was *SEPARATED FROM HIS WIFE AND FAMILY.*

*Article from the Newark Daily Advertiser, December 13, 1904, of Andrew Kimball's death.*

I carefully picked up the piece of paper, no more than ten by eleven inches, cupped it in my hands and placed it on the floor of my car. One motive for rescuing this scrap was to find out what a "hostelry" was. As soon as I got home, I looked up the word and discovered "hostelry" is just another word for hotel. The article wasn't complete because a part of it had crumbled away, but what I was able to save included in large font, *Mrs. Kimball, Who Lived in Providence, Had Brought Legal Suit Against Husband*. The article continued:

> Andrew Coates Kimball, 55 years old and who lived in Kearny, was asphyxiated early this morning with illuminating gas, in a room at the Coleman House, at Broad and Orange Streets. Kimball called at the hotel shortly before midnight last night and engaged a front room on the second floor.

> George Seelig, the night clerk, had his attention called at 2:30 o'clock to the strong odor of gas coming down the front stairs. He made a hurried investigation and learned that the gas was coming from the room occupied by Kimball.

> He repeatedly knocked on the door, but there came no response, and he forced his way into the room. There he found Kimball lying on the bed as though asleep.

That was the extent of the article that was intact. Based on the facts reported in the newspaper, it sounded as though Mr. Kimball, who lived in Providence, NJ, and who was divorcing his wife, came to Newark, took a room for the night at the Coleman House, was overcome by gas, and died on that Tuesday, December night. We would never know if his death was an accident or suicide. Regardless, Andrew C. Kimball died that night and now was forgotten. Because his story seemed not to have a proper ending, I took it upon myself to investigate the matter.

I wanted to find his grave, providing he was buried and not cremated. The article mentioned he lived in Kearny, so my first step was to check the only cemetery there: *The Arlington Cemetery.* Giving his name and date of his death, I asked at the cemetery office if he was buried there. Thumbing through the old ledger pages for 1904, the employee said he was and then gave me a cemetery map on which he highlighted Plot 6 GR-536 in the Rosedale Lawn section. He also identified the grave to the right because his information indicated Andrew Kimball didn't have a tombstone. I guess whatever family he had raised enough money for the burial but not for a stone. So, I was looking for the grave of James H. Erskine 1859-1904.

Walking up and down the rows of the section, I finally found Erskine's grave. To the left of it was just a blank piece of land. I stood looking at the ground, and once again, I experienced what always seems to happen in these situations. I saw a small room with a black, steel-framed bed and wallpaper with large flower prints. That these were the images Kimball saw in 1904 came as no surprise. Visions such as these have happened to me many times before.

What puzzled me, though, was that if the man lived in Kearny, why had he rented a Newark hotel room? Kearny is only a short walk from Newark's Broad Street. That Kimball decided to commit suicide crossed my mind, but then, as I stared at his grave, images and a voice entered my mind that provided the real explanation. Andrew Kimball was returning from a trip and arrived at the Newark train station late that evening. He was tired and decided to take a room at the Coleman House, located about a block from the train station. I'm sure he planned to check into the hotel room, get some sleep, and in the morning continue to his home in Kearny. He turned on the gas lamp, but unfortunately, the flame went out. The gas then filled the room, which killed him. Once this scenario entered my mind, I felt as if Mr. Kimball personally told me what happened the day his life ended.

Without a scrap of newspaper landing at my feet, we might never know this man existed. Probably no one had visited his grave in over a hundred years, until now. I make it a point to visit Mr. Kimball at least once a year. I also feel a personal bond with the voice I heard echoing to me from 1904. Lastly and most important, although these many, many years have passed, you're not forgotten, Andrew C. Kimball. May you Rest in Peace.

# Never a Dull Day

Steve was a man I knew for almost a year, a good-natured guy, friendly and the type of guy who would give you the shirt off his back. Steve introduced me to his wife Maria at a party one late October evening. Within seconds I received a flood of mental images of Maria when she was around eight to ten years old.

## Party Gags

I always try to make a good impression. I know that starting a conversation by relating my images of someone's personal life can backfire and make the person uneasy, or just creep them out. Steve was open to my unusual ability, and I felt that exhibiting it when meeting his wife would be more like a party gag than a challenge to one's innermost secrets.

Steve and I walked up to Maria, I smiled and said, "You were born on an island near Puerto Rico," she laughed and said it was true. Steve said, "This is the guy I was telling you about, he sees things about people and places." Maria said, "tell me more."

I replied, "When you were a little girl you carried water in a bucket from the top of the hill to the bottom. Your house was at the base of the hill. Your mother drove home the point that you should always watch where you were walking and to always watch your feet."

She laughed and said that was right, many times she would trip and fall on her way down. I went on, "Sitting on the road directly across from your house is a 1948 or 1949 Dodge that had an extended body which looked like a limousine." Maria didn't remember that but was fascinated with the information I told her.

I met her again a few months later when a group from my lodge decided to go on a fishing trip. She was one of the few women aboard. Once she saw me, she rushed across the deck to tell me that she spoke to her brother who still lived on the island, and she asked him about the old car. He told her that it was an old Dodge that belonged to their neighbor, who lived across the road from their house, he had a taxi service and that was his car.

## Gaslight

Images and impressions don't start and end with people. I also get visions from places. One Sunday afternoon, Sue and I visited my uncle who lived in Newark, on Houston Street. My uncle lived in an old two-story building which was originally a one family home before it was converted into two apartments.

Newark has always been an industrial city. During the First and Second World Wars, single-family homes were often converted into multiple apartments to house the added manpower that moved into the area to work in defense plants. Another interesting fact is that during this time, the city issued liquor/restaurant licenses to just about anyone who had a few dollars to open a tavern. These taverns became very popular and served the needs of the factory workers. To this day, the street where my uncle lived has a tavern at each end of the block.

I grew up in this neighborhood and these taverns became my first source of income. When I turned nine, I took our family's shoeshine box to these taverns and offered shoe shines for fifteen cents to the customers. Of course, my parents weren't aware of my new career, but seeing their son with a pocket full of change made them ask how I got it. My father found no reason to prevent me from continuing my venture; he knew the taverns in the area were safe. My income paid for trips to the movies, candy and the occasional comic book.

My uncle lived in the second-floor apartment. He often said he didn't like to have someone living above him because he would hear them walking around. During my visit on this day, he asked me to bring up a pail from the basement. His wife decided to mop the hallways and needed the pail. I made my way to the basement and found the pail next to the sink. It was a simple task, nothing out of the ordinary, but it became something more.

That night, as I tried to sleep, I saw first-hand, images of my uncle's house being built. The house dates to the 1870s and because it was pre-electric, I saw workers installing gas pipes in the walls that would be used for lighting. Today, nubs of the capped off pipes are still visible in the hall.

Throughout the night, images shifted, and I could see horse drawn wagons bringing in wooden beams. I saw men with chains, levers, and wooden blocks, moving the beams from the wagon to the stone foundation to form the first floor. These images continued night after night. First, I'd have a repeat of what I saw the night before, then I would get a bit more of the story. Each morning I woke tired and beat.

Every morning I would update Sue on my nightly trek and the latest episode from the mid-19th century construction of my uncle's house.

By the end of the week, the images shifted from the major construction of the building to a scene on the first-floor hall. I watched as a man probably in his early 30s placed a wooden crate at the front door. A young boy, probably around 12 years old, sat on the floor next to the crate. The man was obviously the boy's father. The man popped the wooden slats of the crate with a pry bar. He removed excelsior, a straw like material used for packing. He then pulled out pieces of a gas lamp, laid them out on the floor, and started to assemble it. He showed his son the step-by-step order to build the lamp. Finally, he inserted a wick, and said, "The wick should be short, or it will burn out."

Night after night I saw this man build the same gas lamp over and over, repeating the same words to the boy. It took at least ten days before those images faded and I could get a decent night's sleep. Finally, all the construction visions were gone.

A month later I stopped by our town's local hardware store. The owner was a man named John. He had a thick Polish accent and was loud. When he greeted a customer, you could hear him clear across the store,

"Good morning, what do you need?" I picked up an electrical switch plate and headed for the front counter to pay for it. At the counter, a customer was there with parts for a gas lamp in a cardboard box. He asked John if he knew how to assemble it. John bellowed, "How old do you think I am? That lamp is over a hundred years old, what do you need a lamp like that for?"

Without saying a word, I walked up to the man, took all the pieces of the lamp out of the box and quickly assembled it just like the man I saw in my visions do. There was a wick in the box, which I placed in the lamp and said, "keep the wick short or it will burn out." Both the customer and John stared at me, incredulously. The customer smiled and then said, "Thanks."

John said, "You put it together like you've been doing it all your life." I answered, "Something like that." I could feel both men watching me as I paid for the switch plate and exited the door. To me there was some comfort in knowing that what I learned from my vision was used for something practical.

## Remote Viewing

Images of a woman's childhood on an island and building a gas lamp are two examples of what can go through my mind at any time. Let's face it; information like this is useless in our daily lives. The question is how can this unique ability be used in a more practical way? That opportunity would come less than a year later.

I've always been interested in what is known as Remote Viewing. The definition of Remote Viewing is the ability to receive mental impressions from a distant and unseen target by using extrasensory perception, or ESP. The former Soviet Union and the United States are two countries that recruited people with this ability to use their talents to get information about targets selected by their intelligence departments. Put more simply, Remote Viewing is psychic spying.

The original proponents of Remote Viewing were Russell Targ and Harold Puthoff. These men first initiated studies that led to Remote Viewing in the early 1970s when they joined the Electronics and Bioengineering Laboratory at Stanford Research Institute. In the United States the top remote viewers were Ingo Swann, Joseph McMoneagle and Courtney Brown.

The subject of remote viewing was fascinating and knowing that my friend Ingo Swann was a pioneer in the field led to many interesting conversations about it at his studio. It seemed every time I stopped by to visit Ingo he would test me. Once on my way to his place I stopped at a small delicatessen a few blocks away to pick up a few things to munch on. When I arrived, he saw the bag and asked me what the store used to be before it became a deli? I quickly answered, "a barber shop." Ingo hesitated for a moment then said, "You're right." On another occasion I was at his place with my friend Paula Roberts, the English psychic. Out of the blue Ingo asked me what his building was years ago. I said it was a factory and I could see there was a man with a workbench at the foot of the stairs. Ingo asked me to describe him. I said, "He is about five feet seven inches, with dark black hair and is wearing an apron." I then looked to the right and said, "There is another man who is a boss of some kind, maybe a foreman, and he's walking around the floor. He's about five foot five, has light hair with no apron." Ingo replied, "I see them too; I believe the man at the workbench is named Frankie."

Ingo then asked what was his place used for recently? I glanced at the center of the floor and told him there was a short woman who seemed to be in charge I noticed a tremendous number of wires on the floor and the sound of telephones. I said that the woman was angry and yelling at a man about money. Paula then spoke up in as a matter-of-fact tone, "This place was a bookie joint." Ingo replied, "Yes it was."

I didn't pay much attention to these little tests by Ingo; I considered them more of a game than anything else. To an outside person all this sounds rather weird. However, it is routine for me. You must consider at this time my personal life included a handful of people who worked in the paranormal community. There was psychic Paula Roberts, parapsychologist Joanne McMahon, remote viewer Ingo Swann and George Hansen. George always kept me advised of what was happening in the paranormal and UFO field, he later wrote what I consider a milestone in the field, a book called, *The Trickster and the Paranormal.*

One day I got a call from the Parapsychology Foundation. They wanted me to videotape a lecture on remote viewing by Paul H. Smith, a former member of the C.I.A.

When the day came, I set up the room for a two-camera shoot. Richard Matyskiel was the cameraman videotaping the audience, while I posted myself by the left wall to aim at the speaker. This arrangement always worked well. I could follow the speaker with my camera then at various times dissolve the image to Richard's camera for audience reactions and questions.

Each member of the audience was given a sheet of paper and a pencil. There were about thirty people in the room. Paul had a music stand facing the audience with four large manila envelopes. He said, "I took four pages with photographs from a magazine and put one photo in each of these envelopes." He asked for one person in the audience to come to the front of the room. A young man obliged. He asked the man to take away three of the envelopes and hand them to the receptionist. He said to the receptionist, "Take these three, rip them up and throw the pieces outside into the trashcan. Make sure they are out of the building."

One envelope remained on the stand. He told the audience to concentrate on the remaining envelope and draw a picture of the photograph inside it. He then left the room allowing the people to draw saying he would return in about ten minutes.

Meanwhile as the others were drawing, I turned off my camera and decided to try my hand at remote viewing the envelope.

I grabbed a sheet of paper and drew a bridge with water under it like a river. The bridge I envisioned was old and had streetlights on it. I took my drawing, flipped it over, and laid it on a small ledge next to my camera.

Paul returned to the front of the room, opened the envelope to show the bridge at St. Petersburg Russia. The photo was exactly like my drawing. I said to myself, "Nice job, too bad I can't draw better."

Paul started from the rear of the room, looking over the other drawings. There were buildings and mountains galore. My eyes were focused to the front of the room ready to start recording when he started to pass by me. Suddenly, I saw an arm move in front of my face, pick up my drawing, and turn it right side up. Paul looked at it, returned it to the spot where I initially had it, and softly said to me, "I'll talk to you later."

Paul didn't say a word to the audience about my drawing. I was the only one with the correct image. When the program was over the people left leaving us to pack our equipment. A few stragglers stayed to congratulate Paul on his talk. After they left, he said to me, "I heard about you and wanted to see how good you were." Who did he hear that from? Ingo? To this day I don't know for sure.

It wasn't long before I got a call from Ingo. He wanted me to take him to the Higgins Center in Hillsdale, which was in the northern part of New Jersey. The Higgins Center was a unique library filled with books on topics dealing with subjects like remote viewing and the paranormal. Bill Higgins owned the library. He was a friend of Ingo, but details of their relationship were never discussed. Bill trusted Joanne McMahon and me with keys to the place and said we could use it at any time.

We took advantage of this offer. We hosted lecturers to speak to our friends and invited guests. A few of the speakers were psychic detective, Noreen Renier and UFO researcher, Bob Durant.

The day Ingo and I arrived; the door was unlocked, and we entered. From the back of the room approaching us was a relatively tall thin man dressed in a brown suit. He didn't introduce himself and asked me to sit down in the chair next to me. Ingo moved behind me to my right. This brown suited man asked me to tell him what was at a particular location. He then rattled off a group of numbers ending with latitude then another batch of numbers of longitude.

I described an area with palm trees and an oceanfront lined with buildings with their various bright colors. Seconds later I went on describing a road that hugged the coast and the foreign cars on it. When I had finished describing my vision, I glanced to see Ingo smiling at the man. For some reason brown suit looked angry. Ingo said, "He's got it." Brown Suit asked if I got the visions because of the longitude and latitude he gave me? I said, "No. I have a problem with numbers, and they don't mean a thing to me." I then said, "When you started to talk, I could see the images immediately." Ingo's smile was gone and suit man said, "We can't use you. You must do it our way and our way only." There was no question that I got the target right, yet I was useless in their eyes.

How nuts is that? I discovered years later that others like me were tested and got the target right yet were also rejected because they were not using the prescribed method for remote viewing. I was rejected by the government but that wouldn't dissuade me from using this ability.

# Hauntings Discovered, Hauntings Revealed

Most of the investigations I take part in are not the scary epics seen in theaters or ghost shows on television. They are relatively small uneventful happenings that pop up in people's lives. Unsettling things that occur that can make a person uncomfortable. Such as the odor that came out of nowhere, pipe tobacco used by a loved one who passed, or when a framed photo that no one ever saw before suddenly appears in a drawer.

When I was operating my videotaping company, one service I offered was converting movie film to videotape or DVDs. Since most families don't have movie projectors anymore, younger family members never saw the images locked in those stacks of eight-millimeter films from the 1950s and 60s with pictures of their grandparents or parents in their younger days. Reels of those films that have been stored in brown paper bags or cardboard boxes, hidden on the top shelf of closets for decades, will, on occasion, make their way to someone like me. Bringing these films out of hiding and onto our television screens is entertaining and sometimes gets paranormal results.

I listen closely to the comments made by family members after watching the video. On one occasion, a younger viewer made a comment that went entirely over his parents' heads. The grandson said, after seeing an elderly man on the TV screen: "I remember him. When I was a baby, he would come over to see me." His mother answered, "No, that was your grandfather, and he died before you were born," dismissing the boy's comment. Maybe at times, his grandfather's spirit did visit the boy, but no one in the family was aware of it. I see too often in our society how quickly people disregard any thought of a ghostly presence. They feel there is always a logical scientific explanation for everything.

For example, Bob worked as a mechanical engineer in the New York, New Jersey area. He was very knowledgeable about automotive engines, and he would help me when I was working on my truck.

He married my friend Matthew's sister, Linda, and after the wedding, they lived in Linda's family's apartment house in Newark. In this sizeable six-family house, family members occupied every apartment. The grandfather built the house because he wanted his entire family to live in the same building. When he died, he gave ownership of the house to the family in his will, which made them all owners.

What a disaster. Each of the grandfather's sons and daughters owned a piece of the house, and now their sons and daughters also have a piece of it. It looks like the house will never be sold because of the many owners.

It wasn't long before Bob and Linda had a baby boy named after the father. A few years had passed, and Little Bobby was getting bigger. Linda took on a job, so Linda's mother, who lived in the basement apartment, watched little Bobby. She loved that boy and everyday gave him breakfast and lunch and watched television with him until his mother got back from work. On one particular day, grandma ran out of milk for the breakfast cereal. Woodruff's Deli was a delicatessen that was only a few doors down. Grandma said to Bobby, "I have to get some milk, so watch some TV. I'll be back in a few minutes." True to her words, grandma was back in less than ten minutes with the milk and a few goodies for the boy.

The boy was watching TV and moved to the kitchen for his cereal. As his grandma was pouring the milk, Bobby said, "Grandma was here." She answered, "I'm here," Bobby looked at her oddly and repeated, "Grandma was here." She responded again, "I'm here, Bobby." He yelled, "NO!" and ran out of the kitchen and into his grandma's bedroom. She followed him into the room, where the boy climbed on top of her bed, reached out, and removed a framed photo from the shelf above her bed. The picture was of his great-grandmother. He pointed at the picture and said, "Grandma." She put the picture back on the shelf and brought him back into the kitchen. "Where did you see Grandma?" He pointed at a rocking chair in the living room and said she was sitting on it and was talking to him. The rocking chair once belonged to her mother or great grandmother, and she sat there all the time.

This incident is proof that this paranormal incident was genuine. A child like Bobby had no cause to deceive his grandmother. He was stating an incident that happened while she was at the store. When grandma told the rest of the family about this, the family's reaction was laughter and disbelief, which doesn't surprise me. I guess they believe miracles and visitations from angels and saints only if it happened a thousand years ago but not in the present day.

## The nature and consequences of grief

I believe that we often make a comfortable setting for spirits to either return or never leave our plane of existence. After the death of a loved one, we should grieve for a period then move on. That is the way it should be, but all too often, that's not the case. When an Italian man died in the old neighborhood, his wife would wear a black mourning outfit for years. When she would meet a friend, her handkerchief would appear, and the crying would start. These women couldn't live a day without showing the world their undying devotion to their husbands. How can a spirit move on with this daily show about them going on? This type of love isn't exclusive to old world Italians.

Back in the mid-eighties, I came across one of the strangest things I've ever experienced. A friend of mine named Rick owned an auto restoration shop. There were vintage Mustangs, Camaros, Model A's, and Lincolns around the property waiting to be reborn. Rick had a staff of both mechanical and auto body workers laboring night and day on these beauties.

Then there was Paul. Paul didn't work at the shop but liked being around these old cars and being part of the camaraderie. He got along with everyone and would volunteer to get parts, lunch, and assist anyone who needed him. Paul planned to get a flatbed tow truck and go into business for himself. His father said he would help finance the truck, but he had to wait a few months before he could lend him the money.

The shop had a problem with the basement lighting, so I arrived with my tools and electrical supplies to fix the problem. After seeing me working on the electric, Paul asked if I could stop by his father's house to check out some electrical issues. I agreed, and later that afternoon, we headed for his home.

Paul has always lived with his father and was familiar with the electrical problems he had at the house. Paul's dad was a high-ranking executive for a well-known pharmaceutical company. His house was huge. Paul said the owner of a company that demolished buildings built the house, and his father was the second owner.

Once inside, I could see how unusual the building was. The electrical panels, often called fuse boxes or circuit breaker boxes were not standard units. These boxes most likely came from a torn-down factory. They were huge – three times the size of an ordinary house box. Paul said these circuit boxes were installed throughout the house. This was going to be no simple fix, so I took a pad and started to make a list of the problems room by room.

A light switch didn't work in one room, and a few outlets were dead in another, so we went room by room, listing the problems. The house was massive, and it was evident that some of the huge windows were salvaged from a commercial building.

We arrived at a locked door in the left wing of the house. I asked Paul if he had the key.

"Do we have to go in there?" Paul asked.

I said, "We should.  I need to see what's in there."

Paul said sadly, "I'll ask my father to open the door. He's the only one who has the key."

Paul left me at the door and returned a few minutes later with his father.

Dressed in a blue robe, his father reached into his pocket, removed a key, put it into the lock, and unlocked the door. He turned and left without opening the door.

With Paul by my side, I opened the door. I was shocked to see what was inside. I saw a full-size nightclub, equipped with a commercial bar with huge mirrors behind it. Along the side of the bar was an elevated stage equipped with fancy overhead lighting, including spotlights. Above the bar was a banner that read, "HAPPY NEW YEAR 1960!" Many of the tables had drinking glasses; I noticed some of the glasses had lipstick on them, mixed among the tables were open bottles of scotch and whiskey. There were party hats and an assortment of noisemakers spread all over the room. On the tables were plates of half-eaten sandwiches and other food – now mummified. A thick layer of dust cast a white coloring over everything.

I was now putting my footprints on a dusty floor where no one had walked since 1960. Confetti was all over, and the liquor behind the bar was slowly evaporating. Before I could ask, Paul sadly said that his father and mother had had a New Year's party, and during the party, his mother felt sick and went upstairs to lie down. She died while she was resting.

After the ambulance left, everyone went home, and his father closed the door and locked it.

He never wanted to go into the room again.

The room is a shrine to a woman who died decades ago – a tragic scene for anyone who walks into this house. Do you see that there could be a problem with her soul or spirit moving on with this anchor of sorrow maintained by the loved ones left behind? If there is a ghost haunting this house, would there be any wonder why? Paul says that most of the time, his father stays at home. He suffers from depression and has been treated for it for years. This is why Paul often sleeps at Rick's shop at the warehouse. He only wants to get away from the sadness that overwhelms his father's house.

## The Simplest Explanation

I once met Professor William G. Roll (Bill)[1] at a lecture in New York. He was a graduate of the University of California, Berkeley, Oxford, and Lund University. His discipline was psychology and parapsychology, and he taught at the University of West Georgia in Carrollton, Georgia. He is most notable for his belief in poltergeist activity and coined the term: "recurrent spontaneous psychokinesis."

I was very fortunate to attend one of his lectures, where I heard stories of his cases. He had a basic rule, which I adopted: When you're involved in an investigation, never start with a paranormal explanation first. Always look for the simplest or most benign cause first. If the lights in a room started to flash on and off, don't assume it's an entity trying to speak to you. Check the light switch, fixture, and wiring first. After checking all other earthly reasons for the unusual phenomena, then start to look to the paranormal. Too often, people call and tell me about the spooky things happening at their house, especially noises. They're sure it's the ghost of some dead uncle, father, or neighbor that's trying to contact them and won't leave them alone.

I once traveled to Cedar Grove, a town about 15 miles from me, where a husband and wife swore there was a ghost living in their sun porch, and the noise was scaring their son to the point where

---

[1] 1926-2012

he was afraid to even go into the room, and he had trouble sleeping. After I inspected the house's interior, I ventured to the back where I found a small piece of aluminum siding was loose. The winds made it tap the frame around the window. With just my hand, I was able to secure it. "If you hear the sound again, call me," I said. "Is the ghost gone?" the woman asked. I assured her all is back to normal. To date, she has never called me.

The words of Professor Roll held true. By no means have I become a skeptic. But I do have a fear that I may mistake a situation that seems like a case of paranormal activity only to find out later that it was just a loose board or a bad switch. That would make me, and all those involved, look very foolish.

## Residual Memories

I've investigated homes that seem to have a feeling of heaviness about them. The owners feel sadness, or in one case, a child's room where their daughter had trouble sleeping and they felt the room was possessed.

My niece and her husband invited Sue and me to a family function at a house they just bought. It was beautiful, the rooms were large, and the property had ample parking with a playground and a pool that was filled with water just waiting to cool the family on the next hot day.

I sat in the kitchen sipping my coffee as my niece told us the details of how they were able to get this fine house. As she spoke, I heard voices coming from the basement. It was a man and woman having a heated argument. Of course, I was the only one who heard those voices and kept a straight face as not to reveal to anyone what I was hearing.

She said two families owned the house, with the one family's husband and wife making their bedroom in the basement. Before I could say a word, she said they didn't get along and argued all the time. They divorced, and the outcome was they sold the house.

To someone as sensitive as me, this room would be a constant irritation. At any time, these past owners' voices could surface, making a casual stop in the basement a depressing ordeal. Sadness isn't always the case. I sometimes enter a room, and I'm overwhelmed by a feeling of happiness in rooms that hold fond memories of the past, having nothing to do with its decorations or room color. There is a lightness about the space that makes you want to spend time filling your mind with joyful thoughts. It is a place that lends itself to creativity, studies, or even an excellent place for a nursery.

How accurate are my senses about houses and rooms? Over the years, in late October, I was put to the test. There is an affluent section of a town in Essex County, New Jersey. The homes were built around 1890 to the early twentieth century. These multi-story, Victorian structures were decorated with ornate exterior and interior woodwork with large porches, some with colorful stained-glass windows and working gas lamps. Back in its day, it was a wealthy community of the owners of businesses and factories in the nearby cities.

This section of town has an association that promotes the area and does what it can to keep the buildings looking as they did originally. Around Halloween, the association asked me to go to the various homes to look around and tell the owners about the people who originally owned them and what life was like back then. A member of the association had a clipboard and kept notes of what I said. On Halloween, and for a few dollars, you can take a tour of the section, and the association provided an actor who portrayed Karl Petry the psychic, who repeated to the tourist what I told them days before.

I guess being the real Karl Petry wasn't as good as their actor. As I went from house to house, I spoke of the people who once lived there, what they looked like, and how the homes had been furnished. My friend, the English Psychic, Paula Roberts, always told me to say what you see and don't edit the vision. In one home, I was standing on the third floor looking down the stairway that leads to the ground floor. I saw many men and women all carrying wine glasses on the stairway while others holding wine glasses were gathered together on each level. My first reaction was to say I saw a few people with wine glasses but following what Paula Roberts told me, I told them exactly what I saw. A moment later, I was told that the house's original owner was a wine importer and would often have people over to sample the wines.

I'm sure wine buyers; their wives and friends all came to sample his new stock. When someone is pouring free wine, there will always be someone at the ready with a glass.

Another house we went to was just bought by a couple who had plans to restore it. They followed me through each room and listened intently to what I was saying. I said the original owner of the house owned a factory in Newark, "How do you know that?" they asked. I could see a maid handing a bag to the owner saying, "Don't leave your lunch on the trolley." The man answered, "Thank you," then added, "I'll be home early, I'll be closing the factory tomorrow for inventory."

The woman from the association smiled and confirmed that the man did own a factory in Newark around the turn of the century. We all walked outside and saw the garage. I pointed to the garage and told them that it was once a stable and the extended part was added around the 1930s. I hesitated for an instant and told them that in the garage was a V12 Lincoln.[2] The couple yelled, "A V12 Lincoln?" He ran towards the house and said that he would be right back. A moment later he came back with an 8" x 10" black and white picture of the garage with a V12 Lincoln parked in front of it, probably taken in the early 1940s. They were elated because they were looking for a V12 Lincoln to put into the garage. Putting such a car in their garage would be the crowning point in their restoration of the house and would make them the envy of their neighbors. Still holding that black and white photo they asked, "What color was it?" "Blue," I said. When we left, I could see they were very, very happy.

---

[2] V12 designates that the engine had 12 cylinders.

It seemed everyone enjoyed hearing my words about the previous owner of their mansion, but there is always an exception. As we approached another house, I had a vision of many people on the porch with a small band and lively singing and dancing on the grounds. I would say it was around 1910.

I was surprised because I always thought that people of that era were more reserved and wouldn't publicly be singing and dancing outside. The owner of the house came out to greet us. I told him about my vision of the band and the singing and dancing on the porch and lawn, and he immediately said, "You're wrong!" I answered, "It's what I see." He replied, "You're wrong, and I can prove it."

He took us to the top floor of the house, and when he opened the door, the entire room was a dance floor. The vast room had a highly polished parquet floor. Even though it was over a century old, it still looked new. The owner added, "At one time they had a piano here," and asked, "Can you tell me where it was?" I lifted my arm and pointed to a corner, "It was there." He moaned, "Yeah, it was." The present owner felt that no one would dance outside with such a beautiful dance floor inside. Then I smiled and said that the owner was a stickler about his expensive parquet floor and wanted anyone who danced or even walked on it to remove their shoes, which the women didn't want to do. We all could tell that what I said hit a nerve with him. As we were leaving, he sat on the second-floor stairway, holding an old ship captain's hat. He told us that the house's original owner was a stern captain of a ship and that everything had to be his way. It all made sense to us; he ran his house like his ship and didn't want anyone to mark up his precious floor, just like the deck of his ship, he wanted it to look perpetually pristine.

It didn't take a psychic to see I rattled some feathers with my observation. I never received invitations to visit these houses after that. Even if you're right, in some cases, you're wrong. That's sad.

I enjoyed doing the tours, and I know it made many owners happy to hear the vintage stories of their homes and previous owners. I conveyed information about places and events that were lost to time. I shared images of furnishings, clothing, and the voices of the past.

The homeowners experienced the lives of people whose remains may lie in cemeteries not far from the historic Victorian mansions that were once a source of pride.

# HAUNTED OBJECTS

Over the years, I've come in contact with objects that carry an aura of negativity. To use another, more popular term, they are haunted.

I had the opportunity to visit the Zaffis Museum of the Paranormal in Stratford, Connecticut. John Zaffis was a good friend of Rosemary Guiley, so she asked if we could tour his museum. We all wanted to see what psychic impressions I would obtain from the haunted items on display.

John agreed to the visit, and we arrived at noon on a Thursday, before his museum opened. I was delighted to have undisturbed access to the items.

I was extremely impressed with the collection. The aisles were filled with clowns, dolls, masks, clothing, statues, and other haunted items that were bought by unsuspecting buyers who finally surrendered them to the museum to be cleansed and displayed.

An old photograph of four sisters immediately caught my attention. "These women were horrible, sadistic, and insane," I said to John Zaffis. John looked at Rosemary then to me, nodding in confirmation. When we left the museum, I expanded my take on the women in the photograph. I told Rosemary that those women liked to torture small animals and enjoyed seeing pain inflicted on others. My vision of their evil haunted me afterward for several weeks.

Paranormal activity is not confined to museums. It can exist and thrive anywhere in our world.

When I shop at garage sales or antique stores, I often find an item that intrigues me. I am compelled to touch it, and I can immediately sense its hidden history. Sometimes, I can see the person who owned it. On a few occasions, when I touch something, I feel like my fingers are on fire. I quickly put the object down and walk away.

Over the years, I've come across paranormal situations that can cause problems in day-to-day life. What at first seems very innocent can lead to horrible consequences.

Sometimes out of nowhere, problems arise, and we're completely baffled by the cause. When I start an investigation, I ask basic questions to the person I'm there to see, and the answers often point me in the direction of cause and effect.

When people tell me that strange activities only just started in their home or that they have never had any trouble like this before, I always ask, "Did you recently buy something old or collectible? Maybe something you bought off the Internet, antique store, garage or yard sale, or local paper?" I'm never surprised when the answer comes back, "Yes, I did."

Yes, objects can be haunted. When people put items up for sale, whether recently acquired and no longer wanted or possessed for years but no longer needed, there is usually nothing wrong with the deal. Parting with them brings money to the owner and helps them clear up some clutter in their home while giving someone else a chance to enjoy them. But there can be a risk, so buyers beware.

Some items are especially susceptible to being haunted. Dolls or other toys that resemble humans are number one on my caution list. Their humanlike qualities make it easy for a negative entity to occupy them. A loveable character that takes its place in a child's room and is looked on as a friend may sometimes harbor an evil entity.

One toy that I have found can be a particular haven for negative spirits is the clown doll. Why? It often depicts a grotesque being with a deformed face frozen in a permanent smile or frown. It may have hair of unnatural color and ill-fitting and zany clothes. The Joker character in the Batman series comes to mind. There is a villain with a permanent smile and a lethal personality capable of diabolical deeds.

When someone brings an object with an attachment into their home, strange things begin to occur. Of course, not all clown dolls are demonic. However, don't be surprised when odd things start to happen if you bring one into your home.

Many children instinctively fear clowns and cry when they encounter them at a circus or carnival. Many adults also have that same fear.

Children always remember their special doll or favorite toy. During times of despair and sadness for a child where no one seems to care about them, their dolls may be their only companions. They are loyal and provide love and understanding no matter what terrible things are happening.

I recall when I was very young, I had appendicitis that almost took my life. My Uncle Pete and his girlfriend Anne visited me at the hospital and gave me a small stuffed teddy bear named Suzy Bear. That bear was with me during those terrible days and stayed with me as I recovered. I still had Suzy many years later, and I always felt a special love for that bear. What better place for a negative force to reside than my Suzy Bear? Lucky for me, nothing like that entered my Suzy.

Consider the sale of a vintage European doll from the 1930s. You have always wanted to own a doll from that era. But after you receive it, your house begins to feel strange.

Maybe this doll once belonged to a little girl who died during the war, and she loved it as if it was a family member. Could this toy hold the heart and soul of this lost girl? Could it still retain the affection that she lavished on it after all these years?

In documentaries of World War II concentration camps, I still remember seeing footage of young girls walking with their mothers along barbwire fences, tightly clutching their dolls. Are all those dolls lost? Or have some survived? Possibly over time, a few have made their way to an online auction or a vintage doll dealer. Do those dolls possess the feelings of horror or sadness those little girls felt? If you knew the background of such a doll, would you want to own it?

Another high-risk gamble is tribal ritual masks. People buy them and proudly display them on their walls as decorations. Someone made these masks to represent evil spirits. The tribe would perform rituals or ceremonial dances while wearing the mask, calling out and pretending to be evil spirits. Later, someone got their hands on a few masks and sold them to make a quick dollar. Although they make attractive decorations and conversation pieces, you better hope that it ends there. There are many incidents where ritual spirit masks are brought into a home, and soon after, the family experiences tragedies. You may say coincidence, but is it worth the risk?

## Cars

Haunted items aren't just limited to dolls and masks; you can add automobiles to that list. Such was the case with James Dean's 550 Porsche Spyder, the car that killed him as he was heading to participate in a race in Salinas, California, in September of 1955. The crash took James Dean's life and seriously injured his passenger, the Porsche mechanic Rolf Wütherich.

The story of the car didn't end there. The warehouse where the wreck was stored suddenly caught fire and burned to the ground. However, the car was unaffected.

Famed car customizer and friend of James Dean, George Barris, bought Dean's car and sold parts from the vehicle to other drivers. Barris sold the engine and drivetrain to two doctors who installed them in their cars. They were both entered in the same race in Pomona, CA. During that race with Dean's parts now installed, both cars were involved in crashes; one doctor was severely hurt while the other was killed.

Barris was now a believer in the car's curse. He gave the wreck to the California Highway Patrol, who would take the car on tour, displaying it at High Schools to demonstrate the effect of careless driving. While it was being transported, the car slid off the truck three times, the last time crushing the driver who was taking it off. A student, while viewing the car, slipped for some unknown reason and injured his pelvis. The California Highway Police joined the ranks of believers of the curse. They decided to return the car to George Barris, but while it was on the back of the flatbed truck, the vehicle disappeared and has not been seen since.

Haunted cars are not exclusive to Hollywood stars. While I was visiting a friend's store, a young woman walked in with her dad. They both just stood there looking at me. I asked if there was something I could do for them. The woman said to me, "Aren't you Karl?" "Yes," I said. She replied, "Maybe you can help us. We have a Chevy Malibu that's haunted, and we'd like you to look at it for us." Her father (Bill) said that his wife, who died about four months ago, bought the used car from a guy in town. Both the father and daughter stated that they see a woman sitting in the passenger seat who looks exactly like Bill's deceased wife, and when they approach the car, she disappears. They added that the doors of the car are always locked. Bill said that if the ghost was his wife, he didn't want her to be sitting in their car for eternity. I agreed to look at the car and shortly left the store.

The car was at their home in Belleville, the next town over from where I live. In a few minutes, I crossed the bridge over the Passaic River, which separates the two towns. The address was about five blocks from the bridge, directly across from a church cemetery. I pulled into the driveway, where the twelve-year-old, four-door Chevy Malibu was parked. A moment later, Bill and his daughter, Carol, came out of the house. "Do you see anything?" Bill asked. "Not yet," I answered.

The car had seen better days. The paint was faded, there were small dents everywhere, and the state inspection sticker in the windshield was a year past due. I asked for the key to open the door. Bill went back into the house and, in seconds, returned with the keys. Carol said this ghost thing was making her father a basket case. Sometimes he sits on the porch for hours just staring at the car. Because of this obsession with the car, no one comes to see them, not even family. The atmosphere is so depressing that no one feels comfortable staying more than a few minutes.

I opened the car door, where I found old empty shopping bags in the back seat, paper, and assorted litter covering the entire floor. Carol and Bill had never entered the car since the death. Carol then shocked me by saying that her mother died in the car! While the mother was in the car, waiting for Bill to lock the house, she had a massive heart attack. Bill called the ambulance, but he could tell by the EMT crew's reactions that she was dead when they arrived.

Since that day, the car doors remained locked, and I was the first to open them. As soon as I put my head in the car, I felt the spirit of the woman sitting in the passenger seat. I could also feel what seemed like a breeze touch my arm. I didn't say a word and looked around the interior of the car. As I pushed some of the papers on the floor aside, I saw a small handbag partially visible under the front bench seat. I brought it out and handed it to Carol. "That's my mother's bag!" she said. "We were looking for it and couldn't find it." The handbag had her wallet filled with credit cards and cash. I was surprised to see that there was over $200.00 in the wallet. Oddly, words flowed out of my mouth; "She was guarding the wallet for you."

I asked for a trash bag and cleaned the car's interior in case there were other important items hidden in the mess. She handed me a large plastic trash bag then went into the house with the wallet and handbag to show her father what we found. Once I was through cleaning, I asked Carol to let me know if the problem went away and said that they could reach me at the store.

I didn't hear from Carol and Bill for about two months. One afternoon they walked into the store and asked my friend to tell me that the problem went away. Months later, I heard that they sold the Malibu, and life returned to normal for Carol and Bill.

Haunted items can be as small as a doll, as large as a car, or even as immense as a battleship, and they are real. Just remember, when your life suddenly seems like it's turned upside down, take inventory of something you may have brought home. It's an excellent place to start.

## PHANTASMS AFTER MIDNIGHT

After the motion picture *Ghostbusters* was released back in 1984, floods of self-proclaimed ghost hunter groups throughout the world were born. These groups were ready and able to spring into action with their electronic ghost finders that could seek out spirits trying to hide. Soon, television shows sprang up where men and women explored unlit, dismal, or condemned structures and tried to uncover those nasty elusive ghosts for the enjoyment of the viewing audience. Add a dreadful music soundtrack and infrared camera shots and you have a ratings winner.

Before the release of *Ghostbusters*, if a person thought they had a ghost in their house, they kept it a secret. To reveal a haunting could earn derision from anyone within earshot of your statement. Now, however, it's cool to live in a haunted house, the creepier, the better, and it would make your home the center of attention and a "must" location for the next party.

## I Want My Ghosts!

One afternoon I got a call from a man who lived in Hackettstown, NJ, a quaint town and the home of Mars candy. Hackettstown is not far from the Pennsylvania border. The man asked if I would come to his house to confirm that he had ghosts. He bought the house a few years back with his partner and wanted my confirmation so he could tell all his unbelieving friends of the spirits plaguing his building. It sounded like an intriguing venture, so I agreed to visit his place. He started to give me his address, but I stopped him after he said, "My address is..." I said that I would call him from the highway once I was a few miles from town, and then he could give me the address. Before he could question my reason, I told him if he gave me his address today and I gave him information about his house tomorrow, and if that information were accurate, he'd swear I spent all night researching his home on the Internet before I got there. Any information I gave him would be suspect. I've learned that people believe the Internet stores information on everyone who ever lived, their property, and relatives, and all you need to know is how to retrieve this information.

Rosemary Ellen Guiley happened to be staying with me at the time and looked forward to witnessing my investigation. We drove west on Route 46 toward Hackettstown. We briefly stopped at a diner a mile or so before the town, and we called the man. He gave us the address, and within a few minutes we were there. He greeted us as we approached the front door. I asked him if I could walk around the interior of the house alone. He agreed, and I began in the living room and kitchen area.

The man sat with Rosemary in the living room as I slowly strolled room by room. I pulled a chair from the dining room table and had it face the stairway leading to the second floor. I sat on the chair for about ten minutes just looking at the stairway. I then walked into the living room and told the man that they had "imprints" or, as some would say, "residual ghosts" who aren't real ghosts at all. They are images created by past, repeated actions over the course of years.

For example: If someone repeatedly sees a ghostly figure of a man walking through their living room and placing his hat in the closet, it's a sure bet that they've experienced one of these "imprints." This man's house had them. I could tell he was upset. He wanted ghosts, and I wasn't giving him ghosts but some outlandish substitute. I then said, "Would you like me to describe your ghosts?" He nodded yes. "There are two images I see on the stairs. The man has a large beard and is on the heavy side. He is wearing dark pants, a single pocket shirt, and a tight-fitting vest. Behind him is a woman with dark hair in a bun. She is wearing a long frilly dress with red highlights."

His eyes widened and he said, "That's them!"

I said, "They're imprints, not ghosts."

We then walked around to the kitchen where I saw a man and woman sitting at a table. A young woman stood next to them. I repeated word for word the conversation they were having.

Man: "You're not going to the dance, I thought I made that clear."

Young woman: "My dance card is full, I must go to this dance."

The image froze for a moment before it began again with the man saying, "You're not going to the dance, I thought I made that clear," with the answer "My dance card is full, I must go to the dance." This repetitive action confirmed that the images in the house were imprints and not ghosts.

Looking at this young woman, I felt she was older than a high school student, and there had to be some structured occasion for this dance she was talking about. While I was viewing these images, I noted that the family's furnishings back then were of high quality, which led me to believe they were indeed upper class. I put two and two together and asked the man, "Is there a college or university around here?" He said, "Sentinel College is here in Hackettstown." I was satisfied with the belief that this young woman was a student at that college. I turned to Rosemary and said, "What's a dance card?" Rosemary said that it was a card bearing the names of a woman's prospective partners at a formal dance.

It all made sense to me. Stuck in this never-ending time loop, I felt the emotional pain experienced by this young woman, and being a man from the future, I was helpless in repairing any infraction she committed that made her father angry, preventing her from attending that dance.

This example is a fine illustration of the empathy I feel from investigations. I am removed from an incident that happened years ago yet I'm feeling the pain from this young woman and also the anguish from her mother feeling helpless watching her husband carry on about punishing their daughter. This bygone emotional vision carried with it immense sadness, which I carried for days to come.

After we completed the investigation, Rosemary and I felt that we had wasted our time. I confirmed the places in the house where the owners see these "ghosts" and described in detail what they looked like, down to the buttons on their clothes, yet these two men did not want to believe in my "imprints" and my conclusion that they didn't have ghosts. I was a major buzzkill. They didn't even walk us to the door when we left. As soon as we got into the car, Rosemary angrily said, "They wanted ghosts, and we didn't give it to them. They're probably right now calling some ghost group to come and investigate their hauntings." No doubt she was right; they would do whatever it took to confirm their haunting, and imprints weren't part of the deal. No matter how accurate my information was, it was not an alternative to ghosts.

## Nighttime Visitations

Dr. Joanne McMahon believes that no two ghosts are the same, and I agree. I've experienced spirits that showed themselves to me in broad daylight and at night. Ghosts that manifest themselves both indoors and outdoors and even at times when I stood next to them, believing they were just another person, until they dissolved before my eyes.

It's also known that spirits can have different degrees of energy or strength. While some can manifest themselves visibly, others can move objects, even to the extent of throwing things across the room. I've experienced them all, and no matter how many times I have, I'm still shocked when it happens. I don't believe anyone can get used to it.

I spoke about spirits that have power, but what about spirits that lack that kind of physical force? They are still around us and can visit us when we sleep. I believe it takes only a fraction of the energy for a spirit to manifest itself subconsciously while we sleep, compared to the effort it would take for them to appear physically.

Much too often, people confuse dreaming and visions. Take, for example, Nostradamus. He would write his predictions of future happenings hundreds of years in the future. It was said he would receive these messages through time and space. We do not consider Nostradamus' predictions to be the result of dreams; they were visions.

For me, there is a significant difference between a dream and a vision. Dreams come and go; they disappear as quickly as they appear. By morning they're forgotten. Visions, on the other hand, are firmly etched in my mind. I remember them down to the minutest detail. So strong are these visions that I feel as if I was physically transported into them. All my senses are involved. It's not only visual. I can smell the air, I can feel the ground under my feet, and I hear the sounds around me.

I have a recurring vision, and for the life of me, I don't know why. My vision begins around midnight. I've had it at least a half dozen times. I feel like I'm carried away and taken to a time around 1930, to the coal mining town of Plymouth, Pennsylvania. When I arrive, I hear my name being called, "Ka-roll," by a male voice with a Polish accent. I see a man and walk towards him. I know that he is my paternal grandfather, Alexander. I tower over him. Compared to my six-foot-three inches, Alexander stands about five-foot-six.

We've met before. These visions with my grandfather Alex have become a family visit. On one occasion, I sat with Alex and his fellow miners at a table while they drank whiskey and told me about their job in the coalmines.

This night, Alex is overjoyed to see me again and is wearing a grin from ear to ear. In an instant, we're back in Plymouth, Pennsylvania, walking down Washington Avenue toward Main Street. Our conversations are light, talking about family. He asks me if I'm doing all right and if I am happy. As we walk, I glance to the right of Washington Avenue. Just a few blocks up the hill is the town of Larksville, and Harris Street, where Alex lives with his family. I'm somewhat familiar with the town because when I was younger, my family and I visited my aunts and uncles, who remained in the area. In the 1940s, my father moved to New Jersey.

I don't have a problem communicating with Alex because he speaks English, though with a strong Polish accent. Today, he wants me to meet his friends at the bar, or, as he calls it, the beer garden. The problem is that I'm older than Alex, and he can't say I'm his grandson. Instead, he introduces me as a friend of the family.

We both walk into a dismal-looking bar on Main Street. I speak very little Polish but understand much more. Alex makes the rounds calling out to the men sitting at the bar, saying his hellos with me by his side. He puts his arm around me and points at my chest, saying, *"Ten mesczyzna jest famielijny pszyjaciel."* This means, in Polish, this man is a good friend of the family.

Although my vision sounds like a made-up story, it's not. Truthfully, it's scary, terrifying, and while it is taking place, I am fully aware of what's going on. The first thing I wonder is, did I die in my sleep? I realize that everyone I'm seeing has passed away, which makes me wonder about my passing. If it were my choice to return to the 1930s, I would not be bar hopping with my grandfather in a coal-mining town. I would be with the likes of Myrna Loy, Fay Wray, or at a nightclub watching Rita Hayworth in a sexy outfit, doing her provocative dance from the film *Gilda*.

Our conversations, for the most part, are one way. Alex talks, and I listen. Rarely do I get a word in. That's not bad because the subjects I can speak about to him are limited. I'm visiting Alex in the mid-1930s, and the things of my time would seem impossible to him, like science fiction.

Regardless, he's the most important man in my life. Without Alex, there wouldn't be my father, Walter, who wouldn't meet my mother, Lottie, so there wouldn't be me. The man who is taking me to his beer garden had the guts to leave Europe to take his chances in America.

My impression is that I'm the only one he can contact from the other side. My sensitivity as a psychic makes it easy for him to come to me.

Relatives told me that he was brutal as a father and would punish his boys by whipping them with a cat- o-nine-tails. This whip has nine strands with a knot on each end, a very painful device. It leaves marks on the skin like a cat scratch. Was this story real or just something his sons told to embellish their father's wrath? I always wondered, and being with Alex, I now could ask him and gauge his reaction.

We crossed Main Street, and as we walked down Washington Avenue, I said to Alex, "I heard that you used a whip on your boys when they did something wrong."

Why did I say that? I'll never forget the look on his face; it was as if my words drained all the blood out of his body. He looked at me sadly, like he was about to cry. The few seconds that he was speechless seemed like an eternity. He looked down and said, "Sometimes I do bad things."

In an instant, I was back in my bed. The vision that started fine quickly turned into a painful experience. I immediately regretted my words. Did I sever my ties with Alex? Did I make a misstep that would block future visits? I don't know.

It's times like that I wish my visit with Alex were simply a dream and not a vision. For days I suffered from the memory of this event, which put me in a depressed mood. I felt responsible for inflicting pain on someone from the other side. Alex was happy that he had someone from his family to visit and show off to his friends. I certainly put a damper on that. I overstepped my bounds. It doesn't matter what he did in the past.

To whip his sons was wrong, but what happened decades ago can't be changed. For me to bring up that unpleasant deed accomplished nothing. I always had disdain for self-righteous people, and in seconds I became one of them. If my blunder has closed the door on future visits with my grandfather, that will be a tragedy. If by chance you can hear me, I'm sorry, Grandpa Alex.

# Ronald Devon House

In Catholic elementary school, the nuns, or sisters, as we called them, taught that when you die, all of life's questions are answered and all its mysteries revealed. In the afterlife, you're happy, your troubles are gone, and happiness lasts for eternity. The only thing they left out was the part about sitting on a cloud playing a harp. As the years slipped by, I had no reason to challenge this belief.

I've since learned that life after death is not at all like what the sisters preached in class. As a psychic medium, I've discovered that spirits – the souls of departed ones – sometimes remain with the living here on earth and do not move on. They have their reasons, which we usually can't grasp. Sometimes though, we do.

Such is the case with Ronald Devon – a man I knew for a half-dozen years before his death.

## Family business

Ronald had an electrical business he inherited from his father. He later phased out the electrical work to concentrate on installing alarm systems. Ronald brought his two sons into the business at an early age. They joined the installers already in his employ, and Ronald handled the business end of things.

As the years passed, Ronald's sons assumed the business's day-to-day operations, which allowed their father more leisure time. Ronald bought a beachfront house in Florida and a horse ranch in western Pennsylvania.

As the business grew, his company's success caught the attention of a nationally known alarm company. Soon a deal was made, and the alarm company bought and absorbed his company into theirs. Ronald received cash for the business, and his employees began working for the new owner. As for Ronald, he was now financially comfortable and free to pursue his passions. He now spent most of his time raising horses and enjoying his home in Florida, where he could escape the cold winters of New Jersey.

At the height of the real estate boom of the 2000s, Ronald's property in New Jersey could have fetched a million dollars. It was prime real estate zoned for both residential and commercial use. There were three structures on the property; a small, two-story office building, a house with a small, attached apartment, and a two-story building with two apartments.

The sale of his alarm business enabled Ronald to develop a high style of living. However, the windfall would not last forever. Eventually, he took out second mortgages on his real estate and maxed out his credit cards. The collapse of the housing market caused his properties to lose half their value. Ronald was a secretive man; no one in the family knew of his dire financial situation.

Ronald had a stroke and died in the hospital. Of his three children, only Richard still lived in New Jersey. It fell to Richard to sort out his father's estate and address the massive financial problems. Eventually, the bank foreclosed on the New Jersey property. It was a sad ending to Ronald's legacy, but it would be easier to make the hard decisions now that he was gone. Or was he?

A few months before Ronald's death, Richard's friend, Bob, rented the second-floor studio at the New Jersey property. At first, things went smoothly, but then Bob lost his job and fell behind in the rent. Richard let him slide until he could get back on his feet.

It was about this time that Ronald passed away, and phenomena began to occur in the apartment. Strange noises in the night would often wake Bob and frighten him. On one occasion, Bob woke to see a clear, glue-like substance dripping from the wall.

Richard told me about the happenings. At his request, I visited the apartment. There were no leaks from the roof to account for the substance on the wall. In any event, the gooey substance was dripping from an inner wall. I thought it might be ectoplasm. The Cambridge English Dictionary defines ectoplasm as "the outer layer of particular types of cells, a substance that is believed to surround ghosts and other creatures that are connected with spiritual activities."

I met Richard at the apartment at about four in the afternoon. Bob wanted us to investigate the sounds and figure out the substance that was dripping from the wall. We let ourselves into the apartment.

Richard and I walked through the kitchen into the living room. A violent feeling overcame me; it was as though something squeezed my stomach. Nauseated, I rushed to the toilet and vomited.

Feeling better, I came back to the living room, pointed to a corner, and said, "This is where Bob hears the noise." Richard confirmed my observation. I felt that Ronald was making the noises, but I was surprised to discover that Ronald's father, John, was also involved.

The gooey substance was still on the wall. I went to get a container to collect a sample, but the material had disappeared when I returned.

I kept getting images of Richard's father. I knew that Ronald was adamant about getting his rents on time. Bob was not paying, and Ronald was mad.

Images of the property passed through my mind nightly while I was trying to sleep. In dreams, I found myself standing on the sidewalk facing the office building's parking lot, looking towards the front. I had this recurring dream for about a week. One night, Ronald appeared in my vision and approached me.

He glared into my eyes then punched me hard in the chest. The vision was so real that I woke to feel the effects of just being hit. Ronald was angry and wanted everyone to know. It seemed that I was the only one who could interpret his feelings.

## Fresh eyes and a breakthrough

I was concerned about my friend Richard's emotional well-being. When a family member dies, it is expected that the survivors will go through a time of mourning. In Richard's case, things were complicated. His father had passed in the physical sense, yet his spirit remained a presence in our lives. I could only imagine how Richard was affected, watching me try to get his father's spirit to move on.

Despite all my efforts, I was hitting a wall. I'd sit in the office until I sensed Ronald's presence. I'd speak to him mentally and verbally. Whenever I tried to explain the property's situation, though, Ronald would walk away from me in disgust. I knew that Richard was always nearby and concerned, and I felt his pain as well.

I had another problem. I had known Ronald very well in life – so well that I couldn't trust my visions and feelings regarding his spirit. Was Ronald sending me messages, or was I projecting what I thought he wanted to say? I needed an unbiased person to join me in this investigation.

I reached out to my good friends Rosemary Ellen Guiley and her husband Joe Redmiles. Rosemary was an expert researcher in the paranormal field. She'd written many books on the afterlife and had conducted countless investigations. Neither Rosemary nor Joe knew Ronald. Their impressions would be fresh and untainted.

Rosemary was eager to join the investigation. She and Joe drove down from their home in Connecticut. We planned to visit Ronald's office and property the next day. I had outlined the case with them but had provided no details. I wanted them to have a fresh look at the situation.

The next morning, we drove to the property and began our investigation in Bob's apartment. I was aware of someone talking – it sounded like Ronald – but I kept my observations to myself. Rosemary started asking questions and I could hear him shouting back disdainfully, "Who are you? Why should I talk to you?" Rosemary later told me she felt he didn't respect her because she was a woman. Having known Ronald in life, I had the same feeling.

After a while, things quieted down, and I could hear Ronald talking about his horses. Rosemary blurted out, "HORSES!" just as I said, "It sounds like he's talking about his horses." Rosemary didn't understand the message until I explained that Ronald had owned a horse farm in western Pennsylvania.

We finished up at the apartment and next headed for the office. Rosemary took the lead, turned on her digital recorder, and began to ask questions. What follows is a transcript of the recording.

**Rosemary**: He has secrets in his past that he kept from everybody.

(Joe and Karl were looking at a photo of a horse with Richard's grandfather.)

**Rosemary**: And I thought I was crazy for thinking of horses.

**Karl**: His grandfather's name was John.

**Rosemary**: I feel that John has sort of been dragged into it. I see him standing in the background. That, "I don't really want to be a part of this."

**Karl**: That's what I was telling Richard, I said, "Rich, I believe that your grandfather is in there but he's not a willing subject. It's like he's being dragged into this." That's the terminology that I used, that he's dragged into this.

**Rosemary**: There's something about the horses that's unresolved, some unresolved anger and sorrow about the horses…I feel like the property thing almost is just there in the mix…it's not at the foreground.

**Rosemary**: But behind that is, what I was saying earlier, there's this anger about injustice and unfairness…like, something was always unfair to him…he's always not getting his fair share.

A few minutes passed with small comments being made by Karl and Joe about feelings they were getting.

**Rosemary**: So, we're here in your office, Ron. Anything you want to say here? How about John, are you around?

Some discussion between Rosemary and Karl about the sort of activity that took place in the office.

**Rosemary**: I'd like to ask, "Ron, what could we do to help you, do you even want help? We'd like to help you. What can we do? You know you can't stay here. Everyone has to move on. You'll be much much happier if you're not stuck. Can we help you out? Would you like to think about it a little? I think there's a lot of things you need to get off your chest. Time to let go with a lot of old, unfinished business. It's all finished now."

**Rosemary**: Well, this is a situation with a lot of… it's a complicated ball…a big ball of wax…a lot of intertwining stuff, it's not just the property, it's the horses…I'm just seeing grievances going back in a line that he's not letting go of…

**Karl**: There's an anger that permeates everything…I felt that upstairs when I was outside and when he punched me in the chest…there was just, anger.

**Rosemary**: Ron, we'd like to help you…it's not good to be angry…

At this point is where Joe takes over for me. Joe is about to confirm what I hear, making me realize that what I heard Ron say was genuine and not something I was imposing because I knew the man. This is an exciting thing for me, for the first time I have someone repeating the voices I hear from the other side.

**Joe**: You know, I get echoes in my head when you ask questions…I don't know if I should voice them or not.

**Rosemary**: Yeah, please do.

**Joe**: It's like I'm getting… "I don't want your help." That's what I immediately got.

**Rosemary**: So, let me ask some questions and you just say what you get.

**Joe**: OK.

**Rosemary**: What happened with the horses, Ron?

**Joe**: I lost them. They were taken from me.

**Rosemary**: We know you loved the horses.

**Joe**: Didn't get anything…nothing.

**Rosemary**: What are some of the things that you're angry about?

**Joe**: Everything.

**Rosemary**: From what age?

**Joe**: All the time.

**Rosemary**: What happened with your mother?

**Joe**: Silence.

**Rosemary**: What happened with your father?

**Joe**: I get nothing.

**Rosemary**: (to Karl) Did he have a brother?

**Karl**: Yes.

**Rosemary**: There's something with the brother.

**Joe**: Don't go there.

**Rosemary**: Why don't you want our help?

**Joe**: I'm fine, right where I am.

**Rosemary**: But you know you can't stay there.

**Joe**: I don't care.

**Rosemary**: You're just going to be unhappy and try to make other people unhappy?

**Joe**: I got a "Whatever." I don't know if this is how he would really talk.

**Karl**: Yes, it is.

**Rosemary**: Just say it as you get it. It doesn't matter.

**Joe**: OK, I won't filter anything.

**Rosemary**: Would you think about letting us help you?

**Joe**: Naw, I don't need any help.

**Rosemary**: Are you going to continue to bother the tenant?

**Joe**: I'm not bothering him, he's bothering me.

**Rosemary**: What is your relationship with what we call the elemental here?

**Joe**: He's here, he's just here.

**Rosemary**: Do you use his energy?

**Joe**: I just get vagueness.

**Rosemary**: He might not even be aware of it. There's just this lumpy sort of thing slumping around.

**Rosemary**: (To Karl) Does he pester Richard at home?

**Karl**: No.

**Rosemary**: Just here?

**Karl**: Yes.

**Rosemary**: So, you intend to stay here?

**Joe**: It's where I belong.

**Rosemary**: Wouldn't you rather be with some other people who have moved on?

**Joe**: No, not really.

**Rosemary**: Would you be willing to talk to us about the things that have made you unhappy?

**Joe**: Nothing.

**Rosemary**: We are concerned about you.

**Joe**: Why?

**Rosemary**: Because you're neither here nor there and you can't change, you can't grow; you can't become happy as long as you're here.

**Joe**: I don't know what happiness is. What is happiness?

**Rosemary**: Have you ever let anyone help you?

**Joe**: I'm getting…increasing annoyance. And more reluctance to answer.

**Rosemary**: All right, we're going to say goodbye. We appreciate you communicating with us. But we'd like you to think about all those things.

**Joe**: That pressure's back in my head.

**Rosemary**: All right, we wish you well, Ronald.

**Joe**: (as himself) Thank you for letting us visit with you.

**Rosemary**: Thank you. Goodnight.

At this point, the three of us agree to leave. Joe feels an invisible presence pushing him out the door like a hand on the small of his back. Rosemary takes some pictures. I said to Rosemary and Joe that what I was receiving was exactly what Joe heard and repeated to us. Joe said that, during the channeling, it felt like he had a telephone wire running through him and that he was operating on two levels – one where he was aware of himself and the other that felt like Ronald had entered his mind and was a living presence in his head.

We left the building and met Richard, who was waiting for us in the parking lot. We didn't go into any details of what we experienced in the office with his father. We were all tired and needed time to unwind and discuss what we just experienced among the three of us.

I could only imagine what Richard was going through emotionally. How would I feel if my father died and wouldn't cross over? Frankly, it would devastate me. Richard is a strong individual and is a daily, early morning visitor to the gym. He has the arms of a prizefighter, but no exercise in the world could combat this.

I took it upon myself to do what I could to remedy this situation, and I needed someone kind yet strong enough to intervene in this stalemate and get Ronald to move on.

I knew of a woman minister in upstate New York whom I had psychically helped a few times before, and I decided to ask for her help. Ronald was from the old school and had his opinion about women, to paraphrase, "Men run the world and women should know their place." His attitude was evident during Rosemary's first encounter with Ronald. Using a woman minister seemed like a crazy approach, but I could think of no other person I could trust to handle this sensitive matter.

I once watched Reverend Marlene as she held Sunday services at a small church in Central New Jersey. She was amazing. She introduced me to a different worship style than I had known, having been raised Catholic. I had a few questions that needed to be answered. Would she agree to do such a service? And do ministers do this kind of thing? For Ronald and Richard's sake, I had to do something, and waiting was not an option. I called her, and after explaining the situation, she agreed to help. We now had a plan, but would it work?

We scheduled a Saturday to meet at the property. I was there first, then Richard and finally Reverend Marlene, who also brought her husband, Alex. Before we entered the office, we had a short conversation in the parking lot. Marlene gave us a general idea of how she planned to approach the problem. She asked some background questions about Ronald and the family, and then Alex and I walked into the office.

I never experienced anything like this before. Ronald's attitude towards women and the presence of a woman minister made me feel that this intervention could be, at best, a valiant effort.

Taking only a few steps into the office, Alex remarked that there was a feeling of heaviness about it, and I agreed. Every time I entered that office, it felt like a weight was on my chest, making it difficult for me to breathe.

I didn't know what would happen. My experience with Catholic priests made me expect a fire and brimstone approach. Reverend Marlene's approach was much different. She introduced herself in a mild tone and spoke to Ronald as if he were standing right in front of her. It was a loving voice, the same I heard at her Sunday service. At first, I didn't feel Ronald's presence; then, he appeared from my right side near the room's entrance door. I was the only one who could see him, and I didn't say a word about his appearance. He walked past me and then Alex.

The Reverend spoke about the reality of the situation in a non-threatening tone. She assured Ronald that the family missed and loved him and that they would be all right.

She spoke for about ten minutes while Ronald stood to her right with his head looking down. Then he turned to his right, and his image slowly disappeared.

I said, "He's gone." We all looked at each other and smiled. I said, "The room feels lighter."

"Much lighter, the pressure's gone," added Alex. Now, the office was just an office.

We left the building where Richard was waiting and told him the good news.

There were no fireworks, no pats on the back, or thumbs up. It was reminiscent of the last minutes of World War I.

At the eleventh-hour, the soldiers stopped firing as agreed by the armistice, and we heard only silence, which lasted for minutes. We had our own eleventh-hour moment.

If all went well, there would be no further problems at the property.

Richard could finally put his father to rest, and I could have a peaceful sleep.

To date, I can say, the earthbound spirit of Ronald is gone. He has crossed over. I sometimes stop at the supermarket directly across from the property, looking for signs of Ronald. I can safely say he's gone, and what I feel now is peace.

This story has a good ending, and Ronald has been put to rest, but there is an unsettling issue for me. Over the years, I've encountered many spirits who are earthbound. Many of them died over a hundred years ago, and everyone they knew while alive are gone. For all we know, there could be hundreds or even thousands of these spirits earthbound. Sadly, unlike Ronald, there will be no Karl Petry for most of these lost spirits, who can see them and bring their plight from the past to the present. Nor will there be a Rosemary Guiley or Joe Redmiles, experts in their field who might help resolve their problems. Lastly, there won't be a Reverend Marlene to guide them from this world to the next.

Time can be cruel because it erases the memory of those who have passed from the minds of the living. Old grievances, quarrels, and resentments fade into oblivion. My father once told me that his father had an argument with a cousin, and they stayed angry with each other until both died. Who was the cousin? Why did they fight? Does any of this matter today? Yet, this quarrel could have grounded one of them to earth for eternity, and we would never know why.

Rest in peace, Ronald. We won't forget you.

# VAN WINKLE HOUSE

*The Masonic Club, formerly the Jacob W. Van Winkle House, Lyndhurst, New Jersey.*
*Photo by Karl Petry.*

In 1797 Jacob W. Van Winkle built his house off the bank of the
Passaic River in the town now called Lyndhurst. Not much is known

about Mr. Van Winkle. He must have been a man of wealth judging by the house he built, which was quite opulent in its size and design. Each room had its own fireplace, making the house very cozy in the days before central heating. Over the years, it passed through the Van Winkle family then onto private owners until it was purchased in 1921 by the Freemasons to be used as a club. It's been said that the club was a speakeasy (illegal drinking spot) during Prohibition.[1] Illegal liquor was smuggled into the basement through a tunnel that originated near the Passaic River. Although there is no sign of a tunnel in the building, recent articles from the local newspaper confirm the building was a speakeasy. The Masonic Club of Lyndhurst is still in operation and is open to all Freemasons to visit and participate in its many events.

After becoming a Master Mason, I applied for membership in the Masonic Club in 2006. To join, I had to fill out an application. Once completed, the club members reviewed it and voted to accept or deny membership. I was accepted.

The building had been renovated many times over the years. There's paneling and drop ceilings throughout the first floor, with wall to wall carpeting in the entrance room and vinyl tiled floors in others. The bar room was recently remodeled and was the best part of the club.

If you look past the changes, you will see the original character of the building. There is still an untouched room in the southern part of the building that is currently used for storage. Walking into this room I receive images of the nineteenth century with its high ceiling, wallpaper and ornate fireplace.

Now a club member, I volunteered to help with the club's operation. "Spaghetti night" is the first Friday of the month and I was one of the fellows who waited tables and when the crowd was gone had the task of cleaning up.

Norman, the club's caretaker, lived on the second floor. He was a sharp guy who knew Masonry from top to bottom. Norman

---

[1] Prohibition was the 18th Amendment, which prohibited the production, transport, and sale of intoxicating liquors. Initiated January 17, 1920 and ended December 5, 1933 when the 21st Amendment repealed the 18th.

mastered the rituals and could easily answer any questions you had on Freemasonry. In short, Norman was the go-to guy for answers.

For years Norman was married to a woman named Lee. I understood that she was a bit older than Norman, but the two seemed to be the perfect couple. They lived on the second floor of the club and took care of the cleaning, restocking of the bar, and repairs that would come up from time to time.

Lee died before I became a member, leaving Norman the lone caretaker. Often, I would stop by the club to find Norman sitting at the empty bar sipping a drink, looking very sad. Seeing me, he would perk up and we would engage in interesting conversations. He was aware of my psychic abilities and we would talk about phenomena and share what we'd heard or read on the subject. He was a fan of the nationally broadcasted *"Coast to Coast AM"* radio show that dealt with the paranormal. He was impressed that I was friends with Rosemary Ellen Guiley, who he often heard as a radio show guest. Some of the club's members said he was madly in love with her. To his delight, when Rosemary would visit me, we would stop by the Masonic Club and, of course, see Norman.

*Norman with Rosemary Ellen Guiley. Photo by Karl Petry.*

I knew the building had imprints[2] from the past that would pop up for me from time to time. I paid them no mind. The club had so much going on that this place became a mental oasis for me. However, nothing lasts forever.

One evening, the club threw a party. The rooms were filled with Masons, their families, friends, and children. While the adults were in the large gathering room, the children watched Disney films on television in the carpeted room.

A few times, I had to pass through the carpeted room, stepping around the little ones to get a few things from storage. I noticed an older woman sitting on a chair watching the children play. At the time, I believed she was one of the partygoers making sure that the kids were all right. Towards the end of the evening, I saw that she'd left. The night came and went, and I thought no more about her leaving. I never said anything to anyone about the woman because it wasn't worth bringing up. I assumed that she was probably someone's grandmother stopping by to check on her grandson or granddaughter.

Soon after the event, I stopped by the club after work. I saw Norman sitting at the bar. He was in a melancholy mood. He told me how much he missed his wife Lee and asked me if I remembered her. I told him no that she had passed long before I was a Mason. He reached into his back pocket, removed his wallet, and pulled out a photograph. "This is my Lee," he said as he handed me the picture. I held back my shock because I realized without a doubt that it was Lee who I saw watching the children.

I would soon meet Lee again but under different circumstances.

All the mental guards I had up while in the Masonic Club were gone. I was now open to all specters that were roaming the house. It was common for people sitting in the barroom to comment on seeing dark images passing in the next room; I believed them because I was seeing them.

Often one of the club members named Eddie would sit at the bar having a drink, and I would walk in to see another man sitting

---

[2] Imprints are images from the past, which loop from time to time in the present. They are often mistaken for ghosts.

next to him. That man was a ghost dressed in a working uniform. I kept the vision to myself for a while, but when I felt the time was right, I mentioned to Eddie that a man was sitting next to him. Eddie asked me to describe him, which I did in as much detail as possible. As I was talking to Eddie, I also was looking at the spirit next to him. I described Eddie's brother, who had passed years ago. Eddie was skeptical; I told him that I saw a ring of keys attached to the spirit's pants and with the keys a bottle opener. Eddie didn't remember the bottle opener, but he called his son and asked him to come to the club with his brother's keys. Within a half-hour, the son walked in with the keys, and on the ring was the bottle opener I described.

Lee and Eddie's brother were two spirits at the club, but it didn't stop there. On a Thursday evening in January, I entered the club, and as I stood in the hall, I saw a scene of a woman next to a casket containing a small boy. There were visitors there for the viewing; all dressed in clothing I would guess to be from the mid-nineteenth century. They were speaking, and I heard both the woman and the minister refer to the boy as Nathan. The entire scene was dimly lit with candles next to the casket and a pair of oil lamps on tables in the center of the room. The candles and lamps cast eerie shadows on the walls making the sad scene even worse. I watched for about ten minutes before the images began to dissolve. About a week later, I saw this again; others from the club were with me as I described the scene as it happened.

Club member Mark Tirgrath told me about an encounter he had in the building late one evening. He drove into an empty parking lot – not even the caretaker's car was there. Mark entered the rear of the building and heard a party going on with talking, music, and laughter. He thought someone had left the television on but when he reached the center of the floor and turned towards the bar, the sound stopped, the television was off, and the room was empty.

Norman had medical issues and could not remain as the caretaker. He moved from the building. My friend Jason and another lodge member Robert, affectionately known as "Red," decided to take over the caretaking and live on the second floor.

When Norman left, the entire second floor needed to be cleaned and painted. I had some time off, so I took on the job of painting Jason's room. I was on my knees painting the lower half of the closet when I saw a pair of bare feet next to me. I looked up to see Norman's dead wife, Lee. She stood there staring at me, wearing a white dress like the type a woman would wear to sleep. Her eyes looked directly into mine. I didn't know if she was angry or happy or maybe just curious. She spoke not a single word. We stared at each other for about twenty seconds, then I calmly told her that my friend Jason was moving in and I was there to make the place look pretty. She turned and walked out of the room.

Seeing Lee didn't affect me like it may have others. I wasn't scared, and I spoke to her calmly as if she were someone who just happened to stop by to see the changes that were being made to her old apartment. I returned to my painting and finished the room.

Now, years later, I'm able to view the whole Norman situation in a different light. In my private conversations with Norman, sitting at the bar, he kept asking me for information regarding spirits, meaning his wife, Lee. He would ask about seeing ghosts and what it meant. He would be sipping his vodka with a faraway look in his eyes, and under his breath, I could hear him say, "I miss her." I was careful to avoid making comments when he mentioned Lee; I could see he was in perpetual mourning, and nothing I could say would relieve his state of mind.

I have my version of Close Encounters of the Third Kind regarding ghosts. The first kind is to see ghosts from afar; the second is to meet a ghost up close, and the third is to interact with a ghost. In my opinion, Norman experienced the Close Encounter of the Third Kind. I believe he not only saw Lee but also interacted with her, probably through conversations. When I had my encounter with Lee while painting the closet, I spoke to her as if she was there in person. She walked away as if interactions with the living were a normal thing. She very likely had similar conversations with her husband, Norman.

When we had the opportunity, Rosemary stopped by with a "Frank's Box," often called the "talk to the dead machine." Mark

Tirgrath, Rosemary, and I brought it to the club and asked questions through it while on the first floor. We were able to get a few words but nothing of consequence. We went down to the basement and got more information. We asked, are you a male or female? It answered, "Female."

Without question, The Masonic Club of Lyndhurst is haunted, and I believe it will remain so until the building is demolished. It was built when George Washington was still alive and completed during John Adams' term of office. It survived the Van Winkle family's births and deaths through a hundred years and lasted through wars, depressions, good times, and bad.

Any building that protected its occupants for so long is bound to have spirits. These souls will continue to walk the halls and rooms, occasionally making their presence known to the people of today. Unlike those around me, my experiences with these spirits are more personal. I see them where others can't.

# Point Pleasant, West Virginia

## Mothman Festival

A few years ago, I jumped at the opportunity to attend the Mothman Festival held at the State Theater in Point Pleasant, West Virginia. Rosemary Guiley and the Frick brothers Tim and John, were scheduled to present.

*Tim Frick, Rosemary Guiley, John Frick at the Mothman Festival. Credit: Photo by Karl Petry.*

I'd never been to this part of West Virginia, and from what I heard, this festival was something to be experienced. Legend has it that a winged creature came to Point Pleasant in 1966 and terrorized the town.    John Keel wrote a book about it called *The Mothman Prophecies*, which was made into a film starring Richard Gere. The excitement of the festival, hearing interesting speakers, and seeing the town made famous by the Mothman was what I had in mind as my wife Sue and I began our nine-hour drive to Point Pleasant. Unknown to me, what I was about to experience was more than just a festival dedicated to the winged creature, but rather a psychic adventure that had nothing to do with the Mothman phenomenon.

Avoiding the back roads, I chose to enter Point Pleasant by way of Ohio using the Interstate then backtrack into West Virginia, which borders Ohio. The route was a bit longer, but we would save driving time in the end. In my approach to Point Pleasant, we had to cross two bridges from the Ohio border, the Silver Memorial Bridge over the Ohio River, and the Bartow Jones Bridge over the Kanawha. Both rivers intersect at the town of Point Pleasant.

As soon as the wheels of my SUV touched the town of Point Pleasant, I immediately had an odd feeling. To put it simply, I got the impression that the town straddled two dimensions. I was seeing long-ago images of the town, and as I drove along, my view kept changing from the present to the past. Automobiles parked on the street changed from today's models to cars dating as far back as the 30s or 20s. These images didn't let up but actually intensified. I saw the streets being flooded, and rowboats moving about. As the hours passed, the images became clearer and stronger, bringing with them an intense headache. This was nothing new. I've experienced these symptoms before at other locations when I have become physically ill from the psychic images, but it seemed Point Pleasant was over the top.

It was about eleven PM and the streets were deserted. Sue and I met Rosemary and her husband Joe, and we took a short walk to the Tu-Endie-Wei State Park, which was the scene of the Point Pleasant Battle of October 10, 1774.

The battle began when Virginia Governor, Lord Dunmore, personally led his Virginia militia against Chief Cornstalk and his Shawnee and Mingo peoples. The battle was fierce, with both sides numbering about one thousand. It was a bloody battle with many killed on both sides. The outcome proved to be victorious for Dunmore when Cornstalk abandoned the battlefield and five months later agreed to a treaty.

It did not end there. The land continued to be the site of bloodshed and in 1777 Chief Cornstalk was murdered while being held prisoner at Fort Randolph on this same location. Legend has it that Cornstalk put a curse on the land as he lay dying.

Now, at this late hour on the night before the festival, we were the only ones in the park. Light from a full moon made the water glow in the converging rivers surrounding the park. This may sound enchanting, but to me it was all wrong. I felt as if I was not supposed to be there, not just in the park, but also in the town. I kept staring at the Bartow Jones Bridge, which stood close to the park. I felt compelled to look toward it. The bridge scared me. Later, I learned that in 1967 the Silver Bridge that connected Gallipolis, Ohio to Point Pleasant collapsed, taking with it 46 lives. Given the way I felt when I was in this area, that information didn't surprise me.

*Dr. Sueli Petry at the Mothman Statue, Point Pleasant, West Virginia. Photo by Karl Petry.*

The constantly changing visions between the past and the present, and my psychic and physical discomfort and uneasiness, led me to conclude that Point Pleasant exists in two dimensions or realities. I believe that such a place, with these alternate dimensions, would lend itself to allow such a creature as the Mothman into it.

All these feelings about the town kept me on my toes, but just when I thought it couldn't get worse, it did.

## The Lowe Hotel

When Rosemary and Joe attend the Mothman Festival, they always stay at the Lowe Hotel. The hotel is said to be haunted, and there are reports of sightings of its inhabitant, the ghost of the "woman in white," walking the halls. The hotel sells out quickly, and although we tried to book our rooms almost a year earlier, Sue and I could not get a reservation. We ended up staying on the Ohio side, at a Marriott about one mile away from Point Pleasant. In retrospect, this turned out to be lucky for me, because I probably would not have been able to stay at the Lowe anyway.

Rosemary and Joe had the first room on the floor just above the lobby. We met them outside the hotel the next morning and helped carry books and luggage from their car. I took one of Rosemary's suitcases. We walked up the two flights of stairs. At the top of the landing were chairs and a table designed as a sitting area overlooking the lobby. I stepped into their room and put Rosemary's suitcase next to the window. Within a minute, images in my mind started to swirl. The spinning intensified, and I was afraid I would fall face down onto the floor. I ran from the room to the sitting area where I saw images of men sitting in the chairs and smoking cigars, images I knew were from a time many, many years ago.

Gathering all my strength, I walked down the stairs into the lobby where I composed myself. Rosemary, Joe, and Sue joined me. They could see that something had happened. We all sat for a while until I could explain what I was experiencing.

For me, the town of Point Pleasant is like an active psychic machine, turning out its past images at a high rate of speed. It was like nothing I experienced before.

To the questions, could a creature like the Mothman be real and should the stories of sightings by the townspeople be taken seriously, my answer is yes. To emphasize my original statement, I believe the town straddles more than one dimension. It could be a vortex or a gateway for something to enter and leave. If I had to guess where this portal exists, I would say on or about the intersection of 5th and Main Streets. While the Mothman Festival was at its peak, I repeatedly went to that intersection to experience the odd psychic sensation and reaction to the location.

I know that after such an experience, some would pack their bags and head for the highway. If I'd been in my right mind, I would have. But, although the twirling sensations were much stronger here, I had experienced them before. I tried to take breaks from the psychic sensations by focusing on other activities during the event, such as engaging in conversations with the visitors, occasionally walking around to view items the vendors sold, and waiting in line for a bite to eat or drink.

At the end of the festival, I must admit I was happy to cross those bridges for the last time and to put Point Pleasant behind me. The thought came to mind that perhaps the battle that took place in 1774 had something to do with the psychic effect I experienced. Could Chief Cornstalk have put a curse on the town after the battle? The entire area is full of monuments and plaques denoting the battle. Some would say they seemed to be bragging about the great victory of Lord Dunmore. On the flood wall that borders the town are huge murals depicting the history of the encounter of 1774, from battle to treaty. How would we feel if the Japanese put up plaques and murals about their victory at Pearl Harbor? So, you can see why a cursed land may be possible.

Maybe sometime in the future I'll go back, but not during the festival. I would want to wander the streets to see if I can make sense of it all. I firmly believe that the town has a portal to an alternate dimension or reality and would like to prove it. I envy those who can enjoy the festival and see things without crossing alternate realities, but I can't. This is my life, good or bad, I'm stuck with it.

# Shadow People

Whenever I've been involved in paranormal investigations, I've always felt I had the upper hand because—as in the case of ghosts—I was alive, and they weren't. My attitude was about to change, though, because I didn't have the upper hand for once. This time, I wasn't dealing with ghosts—they were Shadow People.

In *The Encyclopedia of Ghosts and Spirits*, by Rosemary Ellen Guiley, Shadow People are defined as dark figures associated with nighttime visitations and some haunted places. Shadow people appear as solid black figures that are darker than darkness. Most appear to be male. Some wear coats and hats. They are usually six-and-a-half feet in height. They have substance and form and can interrupt light and block objects from view. Shadow people rarely communicate, but many seem intensely interested in human beings.

According to Wikipedia, the subject of shadow people became popularized in April of 2001 when the Coast to Coast AM talk show, hosted by Art Bell, addressed shadow people in an interview with

Native American elder Thunder Strikes, who is also known as Harley "Swift Deer" Reagan. Listeners were encouraged to submit drawings of shadow people they had seen, and a large number of those drawings were immediately shared publicly on the show's website.

My encounter began when my friend Jason Vigorito told me what happened to his father Tony and his uncle Joey while working at a storage facility a few miles west of the Lincoln Tunnel, off Route 46. The two men had a room at the facility, where they tore apart discarded, obsolete electronic gear while salvaging precious metals such as silver and gold. The work was tedious and difficult, but after years of experience, Tony and Joey were experts.

On one particular day, Joey looked up from the workbench to see what appeared to be a black veil hovering in front of him. This veil you couldn't see through, but instead, it appeared as a black hole that seemed alive. It stood in front of him as though taunting him, before suddenly vanishing.

Tony and Joey both saw the veil. Joey was so scared it put him into a state of shock. When he was able to compose himself, he left the facility and wouldn't return for weeks. In time, Tony convinced him to come back, persuading him that it was only a one-time event. Taking no chances when Joey returned, Tony hung religious pictures and a crucifix on the wall. For Joey, this worked because the shadow didn't return to their room. When word got out about Joey's experience, other tenants in the facility came forward and reported to the owner the strange happenings and sightings they encountered in the building.

The story of these shadow people intrigued me. In the many paranormal conferences I attend, a few presenters speak of the shadow people phenomenon, but no one talks of personal experiences because as quickly as shadow people appear, they disappear, leaving only shocked witnesses. I felt fortunate because now I knew of a place where shadow people manifested. As a bonus, it was close to my house. My curiosity got the best of me. I took this opportunity to lead an investigation where I could properly document and experience this phenomenon firsthand and have the witnesses verify our findings.

The first thing I needed to do was to assemble a team. Jason, who witnessed a dark figure and was a trusted friend with access to the facility, was my obvious first choice. Next was Rosemary Ellen Guiley, renowned author and expert on the paranormal. Then I added my good friend Christine Hague, who had accompanied me on various investigations, such as my ghost encounter at Island Heights, NJ, a few years back.

We chose a date that would be convenient for all. We agreed to spend the entire night, beginning around midnight. We would have both still and video equipment, along with digital audio, so at the first sign of something happening, we could start our recordings.

Jason got us past the first hurdle by obtaining permission from the owner, allowing us to conduct our investigation. I'm sure the landlord thought that with a number of his tenants complaining about weird happenings at his storage facility, he'd be more than happy to have someone volunteer to find out what it was and put an end to the talk. Let's face it; word of spooky stuff can't be good for business. Tony supplied us with the entrance door access code needed to get into the building after hours. With all the preliminaries taken care of and the date secured, we were ready to go. We planned to remain in the facility for six to eight hours.

That night, we arrived at about midnight. The parking lot and security lights dimly lit the building. The storage facility has 24/7 access, so adequate lighting of the grounds is essential. There was a fog-like mist that night, not quite drizzle, just a heavy, moist air, so we wore light jackets. I parked my truck near the front entrance door. Everyone got out and grabbed the camera equipment, placing it next to the truck. Jason walked to the front door and entered his access code, but the door would not open. He tried time and time again, but the door would not open. He phoned his father to see if he was entering the correct code, and his father concurred that he was. We waited for about a half-hour and tried again with no luck. Tony said the access code would work on both of the buildings' exterior doors, so Jason and I walked around the building trying the other door, but still no luck. By this time, I was getting both frustrated and angry. I said to Jason, "This is totally useless, a complete waste of time," so we left to try again the next night.

The following night under a full moon, my truck once again loaded with gear and personnel, we arrived at the location. We unloaded the gear and waited for Jason to open the door. Earlier that day, Tony entered the building using the same code, so we were confident the glitch was corrected and we could get in. Jason entered the code, and just like the night before, the door would not open.

While Jason continued his effort to unlock the door, the rest of us walked to the office window that faced the entrance door. We all looked inside and saw on a desk four security camera monitors. We took turns peering in at the monitors and saw ourselves standing at the front door on all four. Each monitor's camera angle was slightly different from the other; nevertheless, we could see ourselves on them. We stood outside the door for about forty-five minutes, frustration and disappointment showing on everyone's face. The night ended as before, so we packed up and left.

I thought about trying again, but I was in no frame of mind to be denied access a third time. Besides, it wasn't right to ask Rosemary, who lived out of state, to stay another day. Christine had already taken two nights away from her family, and asking her to take another night with no guarantee that we would have access seemed wrong. The only bright thing that happened that night was that we stopped at a pancake house after we left the property and had a good breakfast.

The next day I spoke to Jason, who told me, "I drove to the building this morning, walked up to the door, and punched in the code. The pad made a series of very quick beeps: Beep-beep-beep-beep-beep-beep-beep-beep-beep... then a little red light above the handle went out, and the green light came on. The mechanism clicked. The door popped open a bit, and I heard more clicks, which is not supposed to happen. I then turned the handle down and pulled the door open."

Jason walked in and went around two corners to the first perpendicular hallway of storage units. He stated the air quickly became cold. He sensed a shadow in his peripheral vision and felt he was being watched. He ran out, with the door clicking shut behind him.

Later that afternoon, I went with Jason to the facility to talk with the owner. We walked into the office, the same office with the window we stared into the night before. The owner, his wife, and two daughters were there. The wife's dress and hairstyle indicated they were originally from the Middle East. The wife sat on a chair sewing what looked like a blanket while the daughters played on the floor. I introduced myself to the owner and told him we were the people who were supposed to stay at the facility overnight. The wife looked up from her sewing with fear in her eyes. I told the man of our frustration in trying to enter the building. The wife gathered the two girls, said something in Arabic, and then all three quickly exited the room. I mentioned we saw ourselves in the four monitors on the desk. The man said that was impossible.

Jason joined in and said, "We all saw it!"

"Impossible," the man insisted.

He had us follow him as he walked outside. He turned and pointed to a camera mounted on the nearest corner facing the door in front of the office window. "That's one," he said.

We followed him about 60 feet to the other end of the building, where a camera faced the other door.

"That's two," he said. Rounding the side of the building facing the opposite ends of the structure, he pointed to each end, saying, "That's three and four. Now you see why it's impossible to have all four cameras face you."

This demonstration was huge, a reality check that taught me a lesson. If I had to put it into words, it was as if something was saying, "LEAVE ME ALONE!"

It's been said that a shadow person, sometimes referred to as an entity, alien, dark force, Djinn, or the devil himself, has the power to alter electronics or solid matter with ease. It's common knowledge in the paranormal field that totally charged batteries in cameras will die whenever confronted by the Shadow People.

We never had the opportunity to use our cameras because a shadow person easily prevented us from entering the building by sabotaging the access pad, not once but twice, and used the storage facility's surveillance cameras to do the impossible. It sent us a clear warning that it was watching us. Since I was the one orchestrating this investigation, I felt the warning was directed at me personally.

This encounter with Shadow People convinced me that they should be left alone. I never felt so helpless. We were fortunate to be able to walk away from our investigative venture. Anything that has that kind of power could have injured, or worse, killed us at will. For me, I have closed the book on Shadow People.

# THE HELLFIRE CAVES

Sue and I always wanted to visit England, but our work and other commitments kept us from making the trip. However, in May 2018 we finally had the opportunity when our friends, the famed British psychic mediums Dean and Stuart James-Foy invited us for a visit.

We met Dean and Stuart through Rosemary Ellen Guiley. The year before, they had attended Rosemary's Necromanteum black mirror class in Salem, Massachusetts. The next day, they saw Rosemary and her husband Joe at a book signing event at Omen, a popular Witchcraft store, and struck up a friendship.

Dean and Stuart returned to the U.S. next year for an extended visit. They spent several days at Rosemary and Joe's home in Connecticut before travelling on to New Jersey where we were introduced to them. We hit it off immediately; being psychics we had something in common.

*Dean and Stuart James-Foy during a visit with Karl in New Jersey. Photo by Karl Petry.*

I arranged for the pair to give an impromptu presentation at my Freemason Lodge. Being British, their presentation had a special appeal for the audience. They were spectacular! Every guest who attended was extremely impressed and eagerly welcomed a return engagement. So, when Dean and Stuart invited us to visit them in England, we cleared our schedules and eagerly accepted.

I was curious whether my ability to see the past would take me back further in England than the few hundred years I have experienced in the United States. I scratched off the Tower of London from my list because its history is well known. The horrible, torturous events that happened there would make me sick in any event. The Tower has been a magnet for every psychic who ever set foot in England so anything I'd say would have been said before.

Where to go then, or what to see? We left it to our guides as they seemed to have a handle on what would interest us.

We flew *Aer Lingus* out of Newark's Liberty International Airport and landed at Birmingham Airport in England, where our hosts were waiting for us. We loaded our luggage into their Vauxhall and headed for home. We traveled through narrow country roads of the type I remember seeing on the 1960's *The Avengers* TV series. I must admit, driving on the left side of the road made me nervous but

I soon got over it. Stuart was an excellent driver and like most British motorists, very polite and courteous. Back home, in the heavily populated New York City area, driving requires skill and nerves, where a three second pause at a just turned green light could get you a horn blast and the infamous finger of disapproval.

The following morning Stuart fixed us a typical British breakfast with eggs, beans, hash browns, bacon, and potato waffles. Now rested from our trip and well fed, we were ready to begin our tour. We made our way through the streets of the town where most of the houses were single story row houses, with lawns in front and flowers lining many of the paths to the front door. We passed through several traffic circles or as they call them, roundabouts, before we entered a major highway. I was surprised to see a two door 1946 Pontiac heading in our direction. It was left hand drive like it is in the USA. I wished I had my 1955 Pontiac Chieftain there so I could pull up next to them. I'm sure the sight of another vintage Pontiac in the UK would shock the driver. We Pontiac people really love our cars.

Dean said that our first stop would be the Rollright Stones, a Neolithic monument which dates back well over 5000 years.

The origin of the name Rollright is uncertain. Some believe it's derived from the Old English Hrolla and Landriht. The site lies on the boundary between Warwickshire and Oxfordshire, on the edge of the Cotswold hills. The oldest, the Whispering Knights dolmen, is early Neolithic, about 3,800-3,500BC, the King's Men stone circle is late Neolithic, that dates to 2,500 BC; and the King Stone is early to middle Bronze Age around 1,500 BC.

Remnants of Roman pottery were discovered at a settlement west of the King's Men. All the stone monuments just mentioned are relatively close and linked by a well-maintained path. Researchers have determined that the ring was a central gathering area for the people who settled there. Excavations over the years have uncovered broken flint, arrowheads, various human cremation deposits, including an unusual 'tunnel' cremation that dates to 1880-1746 BC.

There's no doubt that rituals were performed in and about the area. The history of the Rollright stones and the surrounding area seems to be never-ending. Each new archeological dig reveals more history to the place. Bones from graves, jewelry, pottery, and parts of weapons from all periods are uncovered.

In more recent years, because of its prime location on the crest of the Cotswold Hills, during World War II, the Royal Signal Corps had a post by the King Stone to watch for enemy aircraft. A bunker, which included an underground chamber was built and used decades after World War II during the Cold War period. In 1992 the bunker was removed and capped.

As we approached the Rollright site, Stuart, pulled off to the shoulder of the road and Dean remarked, "We're here." The site is relatively close to the road, and admission is only a pound for adults and if no one is there to take your money, there is an "honesty box" at the entrance path. Can you imagine how long an "honesty box" would last in my part of New Jersey or New York City? Within a few days, the "honesty box," the stand it was on and the stones would be gone. If you wanted to visit the stones they'd be somewhere in the Bronx, set in cement and now a part of a patio or wall. Once we cleared the entrance, we caught sight of the stone ring. I noticed a handful of visitors walking clockwise around the stones. I was told if you make a wish while walking around the stones your wish will come true.

Dean and Stuart are no strangers to the Rollright stones; they visit often throughout the year. It didn't take long before I was walking around the stone circle thinking of a wish I wanted to come true. After I completed the circle I then backed off and stood about twenty feet away. I emptied my mind to see what images would present themselves to me. I saw blurry images of people in and about the ring dating back many years; but sadly, the images in my mind did not become clear as they normally do and I was left with just those blurry images. I couldn't describe their clothing, but through my mental haze I saw men with longish hair about shoulder length.

Dean, Stuart, and Sue walked toward the open field observing artwork made from straw while I remained near the ring of stones. The thought that I was walking on the same ground that people walked on over a thousand years ago was humbling to me. I realized, although I can see clearly events or places in the past, this proved I do have my limitations. Perhaps testing my ability at a place so old was too much for me to absorb or handle. But this was day one; we had other places to go. I realized I could be rushing things and needed time to take in this new land and environment.

Our hosts had carefully planned several places to visit during our stay and graciously did all the driving. As we drove, I was fascinated by the many small towns and cottages we passed. Many of them were hundreds of years old and had thatched roofs, a common feature of older structures.

The homes in the UK are made of brick or stone, including the inner walls. Their construction differs from US houses, which are mostly made of wood. Maybe this is why homes in the UK last as long as they do. Buildings over three-hundred years old are common in the UK but back in the states, if a building is a hundred years old, we make plans to replace it.

One of the places Stuart and Dean took us was the Hellfire Caves. Stuart asked if we had ever heard of them. We replied no, but the idea of walking through a cave sounded great.

The Hellfire Caves are about 30 miles northwest of London. They are composed primarily of chalk and are set into a hillside above the village of Wycombe. The caves are a quarter mile long and run under St. Lawrence's Church and Mausoleum. Sir Francis Dashwood constructed both the church and mausoleum at about the same time as the caves were excavated.

Around 1740, Sir Francis Dashwood began a project to supply chalk for a three-mile road connecting West Wycombe and High Wycombe. He employed local farm workers to mine the chalk. Times were rough for the farmers, who coped with droughts and poor harvests. A job tunneling for one shilling a day was a blessing. The excavation was not easy; the digging was all performed by hand.

By 1750 there was no more need for chalk. Dashwood turned the now abandoned mine into a gathering place he called The Brotherhood of St. Francis of Wycombe. Later, it was renamed The Order of Knights of West Wycombe and The Order of the Friars of

St. Francis of West Wycombe. It was only later that the former mine became known as the Hellfire Club.

The Hellfire Club met eight miles away at the Medmenham Abbey on the Thames. Sometime between 1750-1760 the club changed their location to the caves at Wycombe.

I knew nothing of the caves or their history before we arrived. Dean and Stuart were careful not to divulge any information about them. (I have a standing rule – please don't tell me anything about a place I am to investigate. I want to get a fresh impression without being influenced by information about the location.)

Stuart dropped us at the site and drove off to park the car. When he returned, we paid our admission and entered the cave. I avoided the signs posted along the first thirty feet and instead descended directly into the cave. As we walked, I turned to Sue, smiled, and said that there had been wild times here.

Today, the caves have electric lights to guide people through the narrow passages. But the images I saw from the past were quite different from present day reality. Unlike my experience at the Rollright stones, here I got many clear images. In my visions the caves were incredibly dark, and people would navigate by candles mounted in clear box candleholders.

I heard men and women laughing and carrying on. I caught a glimpse of a young man carrying a small barrel of spirits, making his way to the lower chamber. The passages were so narrow and steep that it would be impossible for anyone to carry a standard size barrel, so these much smaller, personal size vessels were used.

Small chambers had been dug out from the sides of the main passage, where couples could meet. I saw a chamber to the right where a man and woman sat on a blanket with three candles lit. They drank from pewter cups which reflected the dim candlelight.

The woman was unattractive. Her hair was straggly and greasy, and her smile lacked a few front teeth. She was probably in her 20s but looked much older. I could hear her speak, but even though she was speaking English, her accent was so thick that I couldn't understand her. The man was small, maybe five foot three or four, and his cloths looked worn. The cavern had the same damp smell as today, but I could get a whiff of severe body odor.

In another chamber I passed I heard activity but could see nothing as it was unlit. I had no idea who occupied it or what they were doing.

At the bottom of the cave the smell of powerful, sweet perfume filled the air; yet as I looked around, I saw no one. I'm sure the women who provided companionship to these men were prostitutes.

While I walked through the cave, images rapidly switched from yesterday to today, from visitors snapping pictures of their families back to the dark chambers. Yet through it all I could still hear the sounds made by the nightly occupants of two hundred sixty years ago.

I sensed that strange ceremonies took place in the centrally located chamber. As a Freemason I am familiar with rituals and their esoteric roots. I saw a group of people in dark clothing in a tight group in the center of the room. Others stood along the walls. A small fire burned in the center and cast weird shadows. It seemed that everyone took part in a repetitious chanting. The words I heard were not English – I guessed that they were Latin.

I remained in this chamber for at least ten minutes. The images became ever stronger. The participants stared into the flame with dead eyes. I felt fear – an ominous feeling that sent shivers up my spine. I felt like a spy and that I was in danger if I was discovered by these people. The scene ran counter to my Christian teachings. It hinged on the Satanic.

Strangely, as I witnessed this scene, no one from the present entered the chamber. I was there alone.

Slowly the chanting and images faded. People began to enter the chamber speaking loudly and taking pictures. It was time for me to leave. I walked up from the central chamber feeling a negative, disturbing aura about the place.

Benjamin Franklin was a close friend of Dashwood and it's been said that he visited the caves on more than one occasion. I wonder if Franklin ever took part in the sordid activities I witnessed. He was an unconventional person for his time. Franklin was known as a womanizer and of having an interest in the occult. To add to his mystique, in Pennsylvania he was the Grand Master of Freemasons – considered by many to be a secret organization.

Until he left England in 1776, Ben Franklin lived at 36 Craven Street in London. In 1998 conservationists, while making repairs on this building, uncovered twelve-hundred bones from fifteen people under the basement floor. To some, this discovery was proof of Franklin's occult dealings. Today however, it's believed that Franklin's young friend and protégé, William Hewson, was operating an anatomy lab. Grave robbing and dissection were illegal at the time and carried a harsh punishment. Highly likely whatever was left of the dissections were buried in the home to avoid the risk of being caught disposing of the remains.

I'm sure that Ben Franklin was curious to see the nightly goings-on at his house. Were the bones the remains of medical procedures or occult rituals? We'll never know for sure. What I can say, knowing his reputed personality, the Hellfire Caves would be something Ben Franklin would have loved. I didn't see Franklin during my time at the caves, but I wish that I had.

I glanced at Dean and Stuart throughout our tour, knowing very well that they had their own psychic impressions of the cave. Sue was enjoying herself, going from passage to passage. But I knew that in her heart she wasn't a cave fan and that she looked forward to getting back into the daylight.

Before we left, we stopped at a souvenir store and café by the cave entrance. We got a table and sat facing the cave. As we enjoyed English cream tea and scones, I continued to get images. It wasn't until later that night, while asleep, that those images began to fall into place.

Back in its heyday, there was a door to the right of the cave entrance. Behind that door were freshly made candles hanging downwards from their wicks. Next to the candles were the metal drinking cups that I saw earlier. A young man would greet you, hand you a few candles, and for a few coins, take your request for food, drink, or whatever you fancied. A few feet down, candles were already lit. Those passing by would light their candles from the flame and proceed down the path.

Back then, visitors to the Hellfire Club stayed all night. When it was time for the guests to return in the morning, a man would hold a lantern that could be seen from the main street of the town below. One by one a parade of carriages would make its way up the hill to take back the partygoers.

The carriages didn't look like what we expect from the Hollywood films we've grown accustomed to over the years. They were far from being the beautiful black carriages with gold flowers stenciled along the sideboards, with bright red wheels and highly polished brass accents. In reality, the wheels were filthy with mud stuck in the spokes and muck slung along the entire length. The paint was brushed on with a course brush leaving thick streaks, and there were spots from various repairs. I couldn't see the condition of the seats but I'm sure they were in the same sad shape as the coach itself. Maybe they were early taxis for hire. I've been in taxis that were smelly and raunchy. I suppose some things never change.

Later that evening Dean and Stuart gave me their impressions of the Hellfire Caves, which often mirrored mine. I'm sure if given the opportunity to tour the caves alone or with fellow psychic mediums like Dean and Stuart, I would have clearer visions of the caves and the people who frequented them.

I will always remember my trip to the Hellfire Caves. These visions now lodged in my mind will bring sleepless nights and the haunting images of looking into the eyes of people long dead.

# STONEHENGE

## England

I knew, prior to our trip to England that I would visit the ancient site of Stonehenge. I'd heard the many stories and theories that surround Stonehenge from professors, historians, writers, and even fellow psychics. I looked forward to the challenge of tapping into this ancient site. I felt it would be difficult, but not impossible.

Many nights in the weeks leading up to our trip, as I tried to fall asleep, images of Stonehenge would pop into my mind. For me this is not uncommon. Often, I experience visions leading up to an investigation. My images always turn out to be spot on. What I saw of Stonehenge both fascinated and shocked me. Soon, I'd be at the actual site. I could hardly wait.

I saw many people in the fields, in all directions, surrounding the stone monument. But the monument lacked some of the outer stones. It appeared to be still under construction. I walked among the people, observing, and listening to them. Their language was strange, and I couldn't understand a single spoken word. Then, as I was in the lower part of the southern field, I heard an ultra-high pitched, shrilling sound. I looked toward the monument and saw a large stone levitating toward the circle. Everyone stared at the sight but to them it wasn't anything unusual. The sound I experienced woke me and made it impossible to fall back to sleep.

Experts say Stonehenge was constructed around 3000 BC during the Neolithic age. Over the next 1000 years, changes were made, leading into the Bronze Age at 1500 BC. Some of the larger stones, such as the 25 to 30-ton Sarsen Bluestone, came from approximately 20 to 30 miles away. The inner stones were 3- to 5-ton volcanic bluestone blocks from a quarry in Wales, Craig Rhos-y-felin, 160 miles away.

This information was helpful. However, it didn't answer my questions. How did these early people move such large stones these long distances? How could they cut one-piece stones weighing six to ten thousand pounds from a quarry in Wales? What kinds of tools did they use? How did they move the stones? I thought that my visit to the site would give me the answers.

It was a bright, sunny morning when our hosts, Stuart and Dean, drove Sue and me to Salisbury, the site of Stonehenge. Dean and Stuart had visited many times before. We parked some distance from the visitor's center, about a ten-minute walk. It was a clear day, and the temperature was pleasant. As we waited in line to get our tickets, I noticed the Stonehenge Museum to our right. Judging from the multitude of languages I heard spoken at the center, I realized that people from all over the world were here.

Soon, we boarded the bus that would take us to the site. There is a constant flow of buses carrying people to and from Stonehenge, so we didn't have long to wait.

I could not touch the stones as the area was roped off from the public. Many people pointed and took photos, commenting on their size. Whole families stood in front of the ropes for group portraits with Stonehenge in the background.

I began to walk slowly around the circle with Dean, Stuart, and Sue. Now that I was at the site, I tried to get a handle on the images I saw in my visions of the floating stones. How could I explain the method of levitating boulders in the ancient world? Instead of the levitation theory, I tried to think of how these primitive people built the monument, given their limited resources. I couldn't see how they did it. I was convinced that the high-pitched shrilling sound related to the levitation. An electrical field could have generated the sound.

A very strange thing happened to Stuart while we walked around Stonehenge. As I went ahead taking photographs, I heard a loud crack of electricity. I turned to see Stuart holding his arm and all the people around us stopped in their tracks looking at him. There was no doubt that a sizable electrical charge had zapped Stuart. I looked to see if there were any cables or wires in the grass, which if shorted could explain the cause of this shock, but none were present. I asked Stuart to give me a firsthand account of what happened to him at Stonehenge.

Here is Stuart's account:

> I was walking with Dean and Sueli by my side, Karl just slightly ahead. We were approaching a walkway when we stopped to talk. As I leaned against a wooden post, I received an electric shock. The charge made a loud cracking sound, heard by us all and others around us. I felt it shoot through my arm, it was very painful. For 30 minutes afterwards it felt numb and [I] likened it to a bee sting.

> We looked around for an explanation and there was no reason why this should happen. I find it both fascinating and puzzling.

It seems an odd coincidence that as I thought about an electrical hum that moves boulders that Stuart got a sizable electrical shock out of nowhere.

I recall a visit to remote viewer Ingo Swann at his studio. He had just completed a painting of a desert scene that showed floating rocks. Before I could say a word, he looked at me very seriously and said, "Some rocks float at night." Since his passing, I'm sure this painting is now on display at some museum. Did he really know something about anti-gravity stones? He was truly a man of mystery.

A more practical explanation of the building of Stonehenge comes from the story of Coral Castle in Homestead, Florida. A Latvian immigrant named Edward Leedskalnin, born on August 10, 1887, came to the United States in 1917 and settled in the Pacific Northwest. He worked in the logging business; the census at the time listed his occupation as an ax-handle manufacturer. Because of health reasons he moved to Florida in the early 1920s.

This slight, five foot tall, 100-pound man claimed to understand reverse magnetism, a means to nullify gravity. He said he inherited this knowledge from the builders of King Solomon's Temple and the Pyramids of Egypt.

In 1923 he bought a piece of land in Florida and called it Rock Gate Park. In twenty years he built what we know today as Coral Castle. It is considered the only modern megalithic structure ever built. Stones in his castle weigh from 10 to 30 tons. To lift and move these enormous stones he used a makeshift wooden tripod made from Florida pine and a few chains. His materials could not possibly lift such heavy stones.

He worked at night and made it a point never to share his secret with anybody. If onlookers stopped, he would wave to them and walk away only to continue working after they were gone. In his journal titled *Magnetic Current* he stated that real gravity is actually a real magnet. So, if you reverse the magnetic force with possibly a radio frequency it would make the stones weightless.

It would seem he discovered the ancient secret of transforming stones into weightless objects. There's no question of the authenticity of Edward Leedskalnin's work, because Coral Castle exists in Homestead, Florida and is open to the public to view.

Edward died on December 7, 1951 and took with him his secret of anti-gravity. Stonehenge being built with Edward Leedskalnin's anti-gravity technique seems more realistic than the fantasy logic the educators and researchers are trying to sell to the public. Let's not forget the electric shock at Stonehenge that came out of nowhere and injured Stuart. It may have been an element still on site that once was used in the movement of these enormous stones.

I walked away from Stonehenge satisfied that the shrilling sounds that interrupted my sleep were part of a genuine phenomenon of levitation. I was also surprised by the emptiness of the lands surrounding these stones in modern times. It was a stark contrast to the thousands of people thronging the metropolitan center I saw in my visions.

Thousands of years from now, will tourists come to see where we lived and scrutinize how and why we built our odd structures, and will their educators insist that the remains of Stuart and Dean's Vauxhall was some holy shrine? One can only guess.

# Time Slip

On my night table next to my bed is my White Sound Design clock radio shaped like a cube. I've been staring at it since I slid under my blanket and into bed at eleven. When the digital display showed 3:21AM I couldn't stay any longer in bed and I decided to get up. My wife, Sue, was in a deep sleep and my cat Sabrina, lying in her cat bed, looked up long enough to open one eye before resuming her sleep. I turned the light on in the bathroom and saw my haggard face in the mirror. Sue won't be up before seven so do I return to bed to wait it out? Maybe turn the television on and watch late night reruns of *The Honeymooners* or one of the endless talk shows slotted at this ungodly hour for insomniacs? I chose *The Honeymooners* and a few sitcoms from the 1950s.

These sleepless nights are common for me. Nighttime brings visions of paranormal things I've experienced. This night was especially bad because it brought back memories of a terrifying event that I had absolutely no control of, which could have been lethal for me.

My experience began with the purchase of a used Cadillac Sedan DeVille. I was working as a legal videographer and photographer at the time. My work took me through the greater New York Metropolitan area. Some of the places I visited were not the best or safest of neighborhoods. My Plymouth Volare, which I'd bought for three hundred dollars, was so rusty that I had to store my camera cases in the back seat because the floor of the trunk was so rusty that you could see much of the road underneath it. The last voyage of the Volare happened outside Philadelphia in Cherry Hill, New Jersey. The A-frame which held the left front wheel broke loose making the car impossible to drive. There was no use in trying to fix it. I just junked the car where it stopped.

The next day in the local paper, I read about a Cadillac for sale. The seller wrote that it was in good shape and only seven hundred dollars. I called the owner and although it was already late in the day, he said that he'd stop by with the car. I told him that if I liked it, I'd buy the car on the spot.

The Cadillac needed a paint job but was mechanically sound. Most importantly, it had no rust. The enormous trunk was a big plus; it would easily hold all the equipment I hauled from job to job. I bought the car that night. While I drove the man back home, I learned that he was selling the car because he was running for public office in Bergen County, New Jersey. The car was a donation to his campaign, so a speedy sale gave him cash for his campaign. It was a win for us both, because I got a great car at an unbelievable price. Soon after, I took the car to the local Maaco auto body shop, had it painted and ended up with a rather smart looking Cadillac.

These large road yachts have complicated electronic systems. The elegant dashboard conceals miles of multicolored wires. One night as I was returning home from a video shoot, traveling down Route 280, my headlights suddenly turned off. At the time, I was traveling sixty miles-per-hour in traffic. Luckily for me the highway was well-lit, and I managed to make it home without incident.

The next morning, I turned on the headlight switch and the lights came on. I went over, under, and around the entire car trying to find a loose wire or faulty switch, but no matter how much I shook the wires the headlights remained on.

That night coming back from shopping, you guessed it, the lights turned off again.

I had a good friend named Alberto, who owned an auto repair shop in the neighboring town of North Arlington. I stopped by and told him about my finicky headlights. Alberto was not surprised. He was familiar with this problem. Rather than take up time at the shop, he asked me to meet him at his house in Glen Ridge at six.

He lived on Hillside Avenue in a very nice, tree-lined neighborhood. I arrived early and parked in front of his house. My Cadillac's red leather seats were very cozy, so I put the window down and the radio on and watched cars passing on the main street just a block away.

It wasn't long before this comfortable setting took a turn for the worse. The ambient sound outside began to fade; even the car radio seemed to be losing its volume and in a flash the world went silent. I began hearing the World War I song, "Over There" sung by a choir of men. At first, it was very soft, but as the song repeated again and again it became louder each time. The music in my head was now deafening. Hoping to escape the noise, I exited the car. I'll walk away from the house and car, I thought, in hopes that the music would stop. I walked to the main street, Belleville Avenue.

*Entrance to the Bloomfield Cemetery, Bloomfield, New Jersey.*
*Photo by Karl Petry.*

Across the intersection of Hillside Avenue and Belleville Avenue is the Bloomfield Cemetery. My walk wasn't helping as the song got louder and louder. I passed through the front gate of the cemetery and, once inside, I turned toward a circle of gravestones, which were the graves of soldiers who had served in World War I. Instantly, the music stopped. It was as if the music purposely led me to the cemetery and to these soldiers' graves. Why was this happening to me? All I wanted to do was get my headlights fixed, and now I was standing in a cemetery overlooking gravestones of World War I veterans.

Looking down on the stones I began to get a strange sensation. The stones suddenly disappeared. The lines of tombstones were now replaced by trees. I turned my head to the front gate. It too was gone along with the metal fence that separated the cemetery from Belleville Avenue. I saw another fence in its place. A wooden fence, not a picket type but long timbers suspended on "X" supports. Belleville Avenue was still there but its surface was dirt. All this happened in seconds; one image was quickly superimposed with another.

Maybe this experience would fascinate some people, but it scared me. Something was happening that I had no control over. I want to make this clear. It was not a dream state or hallucination. I was physically there at the site with the ground under my feet and the wind and smells you would find in a wooded area.

My vision cleared and the ambient sound that I lost just a few minutes ago returned to normal. I was confused; I didn't know what to do. All that I knew had gone, and in its place was another world and another time.

Things went from bad to worse. Now, I could hear someone talking. I turned to my left to see a gathering of people facing a minister reading from a prayer book. Bravely, I walked toward the gathering and saw that a burial was taking place. I got within a hundred feet of the grave when the minister stopped talking and he and the people turned and looked at me. I continued to walk behind them to escape the scene and found a large stone to sit on. The minister spoke of the deceased, a soldier of the Revolution, and offered prayers for his soul. At different times a woman or man who was standing in front of the open grave would look at me, probably trying to figure out why this man was there and why was he wearing such strange clothes. I had my own observations; the women wore long skirts that were covered in mud six inches from the ground. Their dresses were colored but faded as if the fabric were dyed with watercolor. Their faces looked old. I'm sure these women were no older than their mid-twenties, but by today's standards they could have passed for late forties or even early fifties. The men's clothing looked crude and everyone's clothing was wrinkled. The horror of the situation was sinking in. What started off as a problem with my Cadillac had now escalated into a life-threatening adventure. What was worse was that I had suddenly disappeared from my wife and family. All efforts to find me would be wasted. In reality I was just a block away from my car but in a different time.

I watched as the burial ended and the people walked away. The minister was the last to leave. He glanced at me at least three times before exiting the grounds. I stood up shaking and nauseated. That scary scenario returned to my mind. The thought of not returning back to my time weighed heavily on me. My disappearance would cause major concern to all those who knew me, and the thought that I became trapped in a time slip would never enter their minds.

When a person suddenly vanishes, thoughts of foul play are always brought up. Your wife, family, and friends are suddenly suspects in the eyes of the law and of course, the policy paying insurance companies. On the other hand, now I was stuck in a period without the skills or knowledge to exist in this time. Mentioning to the people of the time that "I'm from the future!" would bring a one-way ticket to the local asylum for the insane or attract the watchful eye of the law and clergy. These unfortunate scenarios came rushing to my mind in seconds. I had to face the fact that I was alone with no one to talk to. Even my twenty-first century American-speaking dialect would probably get a laugh or questionable look from the locals.

I remained on the large rock in the cemetery for a few minutes. As I contemplated my situation, another sound hit my head, a high-pitched ringing. Before my eyes, I saw the wooden fence change back to its original modern-day form. The trees that were covering the area were now lines of tombstones. In a flash, I returned to present day. Without losing a second, I ran out of the cemetery, up the avenue, down Hillside Avenue and to my Cadillac with the faulty headlights. With keys in the ignition and the engine roaring to life, I headed home.

*Tombstone of David Baldwin, seen by Karl upon his return to the cemetery.*
*Photo by Karl Petry.*

When I got home, I thought, who could I tell of this experience? Sure, I can tell my wife but who else? I'm the guy who sees ghosts or images of the past. All my friends, acquaintances, and family have come to terms with this, but to tell them of my time slip? Nobody would believe it and quite frankly why should they?

Why would something like this happen to me? I have a theory that people like me are super sensitive, that's why we have unusual mental abilities like psychic talent, psychometry and even mediumship. I'll go so far as to say that super sensitivity may even make a person a target for Extra Terrestrial encounters.

Time has passed from that memorable day at the cemetery, but the flashbacks and horrors of that day will follow me for the rest of my life.

Months later while watching a TV program, the narrator of the program mentioned the term, "time slip," and briefly gave a vague explanation of it. I never heard of such a thing as a "time slip." I thought that going back in time was a unique experience. However, after watching this program, I soon changed my opinion. I discovered that "time slips" were a real phenomenon and have happened to others.

One day, I was speaking to parapsychologist Joanne McMahon over the phone and told her of my "time slip" incident while an actor friend of mine named Mary sat near me. When I finished, Mary approached and said she overheard my conversation and knew of someone who had the same experience, a woman named Marie. I asked her if I could speak to her.

It turned out that Marie was a dance instructor and manager for a dance troupe that Mary was a part of. The troupe was scheduled to perform in Upper Montclair the following week. Mary arranged to have Marie speak to me after the recital.

It was a Saturday afternoon, and the recital was on the second floor of a nightclub in town. The bar was closed but soft drinks were available to the audience. I'm sure most of the people there were relatives of the dancers. I sat in the front row next to the stage. Mary was a good dancer, and I was sure if the others were as talented as Mary, they'd put on a spectacular show.

I was not disappointed. Not one dancer was ever out of step and all kept smiles on their faces even during the most difficult routines. When it was all over, the crowd stepped up to the stage and congratulated the dancers. I stayed behind as one by one the room emptied until just a handful remained.

Mary introduced me and I invited Marie to sit at my table. Mary walked away to join her mother who was waiting at the door.

Marie had a straight, no nonsense personality. She knew why I was there and was noticeably bothered by recalling her story to a stranger. I briefly told her of my experience at the cemetery and the fear I still have of it to this day.

She looked directly into my eyes and gave her account of her "time slip." Her dancers put on a show at an old theater in Vienna, Austria. The audience was very taken by their performance and wanted to meet the dancers in person. Everyone agreed to meet at the restaurant next to the theater.

Marie told the dancers to go on ahead and she would collect and pack the costumes and join them later. Soon, Marie was alone collecting the costumes and draping them over her arm. She walked to the off-stage door that led to the dressing rooms and where their packing boxes were stored.

Marie opened the door and saw the dressing room filled with men and women dressed in clothing from the 1700s. She saw women with powdered wigs in long dresses with narrow "corseted" waists. Marie walked into the room and the women stared at her almost in horror. Marie was wearing jeans and the women stepped aside giving her a wide path. Murmuring erupted with these women mixed with gasps. The storage boxes were no longer there, and the dressing rooms now looked completely different. It was as if she was in another theater. Marie now realized she had been transported back a few hundred years. The women started to follow her as if she was a sideshow freak. She threw the costumes at the wall and ran out a side door exiting the back of the building. Her head felt as if it was in a vice with pain radiating throughout her body.

As quickly as it came, the feeling was gone. Marie was back. She went to the restaurant but didn't have the nerve to tell anyone what just happened to her. It took her over a year to tell anyone about her episode.

I could feel she had the same emotions and fears as I had. After she finished her story, she excused herself and left. It was obvious that her recalling the story was just as painful for her as it was for me.

Years have passed since my "time slip" and I still suffer from its effects. It's the unanswered questions that haunt me. The most terrifying one is, what would have happened if I had remained in that time and not returned? That is the ongoing nightmare that still wakes me in the middle of the night and jars me at quiet times during the day. It may sound trivial but the knowledge of being sent to a time over two hundred years ago and to interact with the population that died so many years before my birth is unsettling.

In short, it's living with the dead.   Since then, I have researched the "time slip" phenomena. Some will acknowledge the incident but won't discuss it, and I found only a few others who will. What's worrisome is the possibilities of a "time slip" that we don't know. Are there some who went back in time and couldn't return? If so, how many missing people have fallen victim to this?

It took years for me to gain the courage to re-enter the Bloomfield Cemetery and to stand at the grave of the man I saw being buried.  I know now that his name was David Baldwin who died on April 28, 1810.  In front of this tombstone was a recently placed marker identifying him as being a Revolutionary War soldier. I hear the echo of the preacher's words at the burial, "soldier of the Revolution."

This two hundred-plus-year-old stone is well worn and is slowly breaking apart. It's my hope that some time in the future they'll restore and preserve it for future generations to see.

# Walking Through Time

*You never know what doors are going to open up and why they are going to open up. You've got to be ready to walk through them.*

*-Lester Holt*

A photograph is an image frozen in time.

The first photograph dates to 1826 and was taken by Frenchman Joseph Niepce. That first photo was a blurry image of a view from his estate's second floor window in the Burgundy region of France. As long as this photograph exists, we can hold in our hand that split second of time from 1826.

Understanding photography and cinematography as we do today, we can easily explain the techniques of recording both visually and audibly, but, once the images are stored on celluloid, or digitally, we have captured time.

Let's not forget the human brain. At any time, we can reach into our memory without benefit of external means and see our past up to our present time.

Imagine that without warning, you find yourself stepping back into time where today disappears and you're viewing a previous time, a time before your birth. You access these visions without the use of any mechanical or electronic device. Sound impossible? I can tell you it's a real phenomenon and something I've lived with for many years.

What some may call a magical ability is also called retrocognition with a touch of psychometry. According to Wikipedia, "Retrocognition, also known as postcognition or hindsight, from the Latin retro meaning backward, behind and cognition meaning knowing, describes knowledge of a past event which could not have been learned or inferred by normal means. The term was coined by Frederic W. H. Myers."

Wikipedia also defines psychometry as "the supposed ability to discover facts about an event or person by touching inanimate objects associated with them." For example, if I hold a watch or a ring, there is a good possibility that I can tell you what the person who wore it looked like or even where they bought it. Aside from the visual aspect, I can also feel the emotions stored within it. I have demonstrated this many times with remarkable accuracy. I am cautious in demonstrating this phenomenon in mixed company because it will amaze the viewers and can quickly escalate into a full-blown "carnival" act.

As a regular visitor at the Parapsychology Foundation, I had the opportunity to take part in experiments testing my psychic abilities. To speak of these abilities openly requires proof of their authenticity, so what better place to do this than at the Foundation?

To test my psychometric skill, arrangements were made with a professor named Brian, from the University of Maryland, and Kevin, a professor from the University of California's Los Angeles campus. They brought various pieces of jewelry and other items, wanting me to give whatever information I could derive from touching them.

We sat at a wooden table on the building's second floor. I faced Brian directly, with Kevin seated to my right. Brian reached into a cloth bag and took out various pieces of jewelry, placing them on the table. The first was a ring. I picked it up and held it in my right hand for a moment. I looked up at Brian and said, "This belonged to a short woman who wore a simple housedress and spoke broken English."

Brian confirmed that the ring was his grandmother's and that my description was right on target.

The second object was a man's wristwatch. The moment I touched it I thought my heart would explode. I never felt so much emotional pain as I did with that watch.

I said, "Whoever owns this watch is going through a traumatic time. He is in constant pain that's never-ending and is pre-occupied in fixing a bad situation."

Brian cast a surprised look at Kevin then pointed to the next piece of jewelry.

I raised the watch to my eye level and said, "Wait, what about this?"

Brian and Kevin both looked at the new item, obviously wanting me to move on with the experiment.

I said sternly, "I'm devastated by this."

"The watch belongs to Tony," Brian finally said. "He's from California. He came here today with Kevin and is downstairs calling his wife. She wants a divorce. He's going through hell with all of this and wants her to stay with him."

For me, the testing was over. Moving on was like asking a man with a wounded leg to run a marathon. No matter how I tried to concentrate on the other objects placed in front of me, my attention reverted to the watch.

Tony eventually made his way to the room. Brian, Kevin, and I could see he had been crying. Brian asked if he'd like to join us, but Tony answered that he'd just wait for us on the first floor.

The session as planned by the professors didn't work out as expected. Testing of the paranormal is not an exact science, which is why it's called paranormal. I never found out what happened to Tony when he returned to California. I wished him well.

## Witness to a burial

*Mary Stillwell Monument. Photo by Karl Petry.*

Located in Newark, New Jersey, and not far from my home is the Mount Pleasant Cemetery. Many famous people are buried there, including inventors, congressmen, and senators. Even Peter Ballantine, the founder of Ballantine Beer, rests in these hallowed Newark grounds. The cemetery is listed on the federal National Register of Historic Places and the New Jersey Register.

Hearing so much about this famous cemetery, I decided to visit it. I drove through the winding roads looking at all the family mausoleums lining the edges of this massive graveyard, along with centuries-old tombstones.

As I passed one of the larger monuments, the name Edison caught my eye. I parked the car and then walked to the stone. The engraving said, "Mary Stilwell, the first wife of inventor, Thomas Edison." I knew nothing about this woman, so I pulled out my iPhone to google the details.

Mary was born in 1855 and died on August 9, 1884. She bore three children: Marion, in 1872; Thomas, in 1876; and William, in 1878. She died just one month before her 29th birthday, with the cause of death listed as "congestion of the brain."

Still standing next to her large tombstone, I felt myself leave the present and enter a past time. (This has happened to me many times. It starts when the ambient sounds of the area begin to disappear.) Many of the tombstones that were there only a few moments ago faded away. I found myself standing next to a tent with a freshly dug hole, whose dirt was covered by a tarp. Facing the hole appeared many impeccably dressed people with more arriving. As the carriages dropped off people at the gravesite, a young man then took the empty carriages to a waiting area about 100 feet from the grave. It was hot, and the smells of the horses permeated the area. Worst of all were the flies buzzing around all the mourners.

Then, as though on cue, the crowd turned to see a small, black coach make its way to the grave. A young man I recognized from photos as Thomas Edison stepped out, along with two other smartly dressed gentlemen. As the minister approached the grave, the sounds of the present returned and the images of the past quickly dissolved. In a flash, the monument to Mary Stilwell stood in place of the tent. Everyone who was there on that date is of course gone now, and probably many of them are buried there as well.

Something about cemeteries seems to transmit psychic energy. I'm not saying, "haunted." Perhaps some would interpret the phenomenon as a haunting; however, I prefer "psychic happening."

In crowded metropolitan areas throughout the country, cemeteries are both old and large. The Holy Cross Cemetery in North Arlington, near me, is seven tenths of a mile long on just one side. Each stone marks a death, a burial, and mourners who were there to bid their farewells. That energy is cast into the air and especially into the ground. Which brings us back to psychometry and the ability of an object (the ground) to hold images and emotions. Multiply that energy by the thousands of burials and it becomes a powerhouse of psychic energy.

These psychic happenings are not rare for me. At certain times of the year these images are more frequent and stronger than at other times. The images come in the strongest in the winter or fall. Summer is the most difficult, followed closely by Spring. The bright colors of grass, trees, and the hot sun put a type of shield in front of me, repelling my efforts to receive the images.

Reflecting on that day at Mary Stilwell's burial, at least for a brief time, my ability allowed me to visit this site in 1884. Sadly, I was unable to identify the people who attended. There were children of all ages mixed with the women and men. I'll never know if the few children who stood around Thomas Edison were his children. I should mention – and this is important – that during a retrocognition visitation such as this one, you aren't physically there. For all intents and purposes, you are a ghost, or, to quote my own theory, you "piggyback" on someone who was there.

For example, suppose a man named John Smith was at the Edison gravesite that day. Through retrocognition, you are propelled back to that date. Your mind blends into John's body, and you experience all his senses for that moment. This sounds far out, I know; however, the theory pieces together all the loose ends of the phenomenon.

These visions are not new to me; I've experienced similar events like these many times in my life. But are these visions accurate? Could it be my imagination gone wild? Let me assure you they are accurate. Here is just one example that confirms it.

I once received a flyer from the local high school that offered adult night classes on various subjects. The cost was about a hundred dollars for the six-week course that met once a week. In addition to classes in photography, basic accounting, and computer science, this particular year included a course in parapsychology. I decided to enroll in it.

The class gave us an understanding and broad view of the subject, covering topics such as ESP (Extra Sensory Perception), ghosts, psychics, and séances. For the latter, the teacher wanted us to have a firsthand experience of how a séance is conducted. She asked us to sit at a large, round table holding the hand of the person on either side, thus forming a handheld circle. She would call on each of us to name someone who had died, such as a family member, to see if we had any response.

The woman to my left whose hand I was to hold was a little nervous about this. Within seconds after touching this woman's hand the ambient sounds of the room began to disappear, and I was mentally transported to a room at a funeral home. I saw before me a young woman with strange-looking hair lying in a pure white casket. Suddenly, a few men in the room began throwing fists and yelling at each other in a foreign language.

While I was experiencing all this, the teacher continued calling on the students for their turn to name a loved one who had passed. Still focused on something far away from the classroom, I was oblivious. Then I heard her say my name, "Karl!"

The sound of my name startled me and brought me back from my vision to the classroom. I told the others I had a vision of being at a funeral wake and described the white casket and the fight taking place among the young men who were there.

The class just stared at me.

Then I described the young woman with the strange-looking hair lying in the casket.

Everyone at the table, including the teacher, turned to the woman seated to my left, whose hand I still held. She looked about to go into shock.

"That is my sister," she said. "She died a month ago, from cancer. We're Portuguese, and we had her body flown to Portugal so she could be buried there. Her casket was white, and my stupid cousins got into a big fight at the funeral parlor." She hesitated, and then turned to me and said, "Because of the cancer, she wore a wig."

After class, the woman waited for me outside the school and asked how I knew about what happened to her sister.

After gathering my thoughts, I said in a soft voice, "It's just something I can do."

Without another word, she gave a nod of acknowledgement and walked away.

When I went to class the following week, she was not there. I knew I had spooked the others, too, because they kept their distance.

That was my last class.

## Gettysburg

For years, Gettysburg has been the "go-to" place for paranormal conferences, probably because of the many ghost sightings people have encountered over the years. Rosemary and I were presenting at one such conference.

This was my first time in Gettysburg, with the bonus that I was with Rosemary Ellen Guiley, the paranormal literary superstar. Rosemary had written many books on ghosts, including the famed Encyclopedia of Ghosts and Spirits, making her the ultimate authority on the subject.

Gettysburg was the site of the famous Civil War battle that took place from July 1 to 3, 1863. The Southern forces of General Robert E. Lee's Confederate Army planned to invade the North, threatening Harrisburg, Philadelphia, and Washington, D.C. If Lee's plan were successful, it would force negotiations with the United States' government, which then would be forced to give the South its independence. Not by plan or design but by sheer chance, both armies clashed at this small Pennsylvania railroad town. It was General Robert E. Lee's Southern Army versus General G. Meade's Northern Army.

When the battle was over, 51,112 soldiers were killed, wounded, captured, or listed as missing. General Lee's army lost the battle and retreated to Virginia, never to invade the North again. Over 150 years have passed, and the grounds at Gettysburg remain solemn and attract visitors from around the world. The National Park Service with its Law Enforcement Rangers govern the battlefields and surrounding historic areas. Most of the town retains the appearance of its mid-nineteenth century past, except for a few massive hotels built to handle the thousands who visit Gettysburg yearly.

Our conference was to start in the afternoon, so Rosemary and I walked around town that morning. We soon came to the Jennie Wade House, located at 548 Baltimore Street. During the battle, twenty-year-old Jennie was kneading dough in her kitchen when a rifle bullet passed through two doors, killing her. She was the only direct civilian casualty of the battle.

Tours of the house are very popular. The tour guides boast that the interior was preserved and authentically furnished, just as it was back in July of 1863. Since we arrived at the house two hours before the tours began, Rosemary asked security if they would allow us inside for our own tour. They knew Rosemary, and without hesitation unlocked the door and let us in.

I stepped inside this rather small, dark house, crude by today's standards. I walked around the first floor for a few minutes and then I felt the present day start to shift, and I regressed to 1863. I immediately noticed the heavy smell of dust. I turned to the front door and saw it opening. There was no knock; it just opened. In the doorway stood a Union officer. Behind him on the street, soldiers and horses passing by stirred up thick clouds of dust.

I sensed Jennie entering the room and standing about ten feet in front of the officer.

"I'm sorry," the officer said. "I didn't know anyone was in here." He turned and walked out.

I started speaking non-stop about what was happening around me, pointing and describing the room as it was in 1863. Then the 1863 visions began to fade and the images of today slowly returned. As the images interfaced with each other, I noticed the wallpaper's flower pattern was not the same. The bed was now farther away from the kitchen and positioned sideways, and a few of the kitchen cabinets were replaced. Still in my vision transition, I walked up the stairs to the second floor and called out the discrepancies one by one as I circled the floor.

When I returned to the first floor, the old images faded completely, and I was back. Before I could say a word to Rosemary, a Ranger walked in. Rosemary introduced me then told him about the images I got from the house. As she spoke, the Ranger didn't say a word but kept glancing at me from under his wide-brimmed hat.

Rosemary asked, "Does what he said make sense to you?"

"Everything he said was true," the Ranger replied. "We had to change the furniture around and position things differently because we added central air conditioning for the tourists."

That admission by the Ranger didn't affect me as much as when he turned to me and said, "You seem to know so much about this house, would you like to be our guide for the next tour?"

Wow! What a great offer. I quickly accepted and became the official tour guide for the Jennie Wade House, at least for one tour. How good is that?

You might consider me lucky to have this unusual ability to travel to a different time and see things in fine detail. But how do I feel about this? Well, when I'm experiencing it, I feel like an uninvited guest.

By touching Tony's watch, I felt his sorrow and pain, but was helpless to assist with his personal problem. The pain stayed with me for days. It's impossible for me to shake off the experience until it runs its course.

The impromptu séance in the high school class where I recalled and then shared in detail the pain and suffering my classmate endured with the passing of her sister accomplished nothing. Speaking openly to the class about what I experienced made worse the sad memory of this woman's sister's passing.

The cemetery visit to Mary Stilwell's grave made me an onlooker to an historic burial. I felt like a nosy person hoping to catch a glimpse of celebrities, which is far from my real personality. The uneasiness of that vision stays with me even today.

My journey to Gettysburg's Jennie Wade House made me a witness to the woman's final day of life, and I experienced the frustration of being unable to warn her of her pending doom.

For any individual who possesses the retrocognition ability, remember, it comes at a price. There is no medicine or advisor who can ease the effects of its aftermath.

# Closing Thoughts

Right now, over six billion people are walking the earth, and just like snowflakes, no two of us are alike. We should celebrate the fact that each of us is unique. Our lives are enhanced by the diversity surrounding us, our varied styles of clothing, hairstyles, languages, music, religious and social beliefs. Wouldn't life on earth be boring if we were just a society of generic clones?

Over the years, I've been awed by people who excelled in abilities that I lack. For example, my brother-in-law, Ed, can tackle any plumbing problem with confidence and get the job fixed in record time. On the other hand, I can turn a simple leak into a flood that would impress Noah. Each of us has a unique skill; it's only a matter of finding out what it is.

It was a long time before I realized that I had an aptitude for clairvoyance, extrasensory perception, and precognition. It took me years to understand these terms and match them to my talents. I always asked myself, why do I have these strange abilities? That question was answered on a Thursday afternoon in 2006 while visiting my Aunt Eleanor, hospitalized for advanced cancer at the Mountainside Hospital in Glen Ridge, NJ. Sadly, her condition had gotten worse, and this would be the last day before she died. As I sat next to her bed, she turned to me and said that her mother, Karolina had the same psychic powers that I had. She said that when my grandmother was a young woman in Europe, people came from miles around to see her; they all believed she was blessed with such an amazing gift from God. After so many years, I finally received the answer to my question. I obtained my gift through heredity.

I welcomed this verification, but unfortunately, it was long in coming. At first, when I mentioned to anyone about my paranormal skills, I was met with ridicule and doubt. It was most hurtful when that ridicule came from family. As time went on, I met people who understood what I was going through. They were well-versed in the phenomena and helped me cope and expand these attributes.

Thankfully I had help from some very kind and knowledgeable people; parapsychologist Dr. Joanne D.S. McMahon, New York's famed psychic Paula Roberts ("The English Psychic"), author Rosemary Ellen Guiley who wrote the book on everything paranormal, and healer Pamela Kramer. They understood what I was going through and always answered the many inquiries I had.

As time went on, the tables seemed to turn in my favor. No longer was I going through life as one of the walking wounded. I embraced what I was rather than retreat within myself.

I began to make appearances on radio and television and spoke at paranormal conferences. Through these conferences, I met others who were like me. For those in the audience, they had someone presenting who understood their plight. After my presentation, they would speak to me privately, wanting to share details of their particular "gift" with me.

If you discover that you have one or more of these unusual "gifts," life will offer you a choice of many paths. Living with your gifts can be stressful, and you may want to seek relief by speaking with a psychiatrist or psychologist. Be careful about who you choose because most of these professionals don't believe in the paranormal, and to talk about it or try to convince a non-believer would be in vain. Of course, not all mental health professionals are in lockstep in their belief about the paranormal. In time you'll find someone who takes paranormal abilities seriously and being able to share your inner feelings with a therapist may be an excellent path for you.

Accuracy in this field has its danger too. One thing to remember, people are emotionally fragile. They can cope with a fool and laugh at their antics, but when that fool says something that turns out to be accurate, the laughs are replaced with blatant fear and hate.

Years ago, Jeron Criswell King was an entertainer who was known by his stage name of The Amazing Criswell. He was known for his wild predictions. In his 1968 book, CRISWELL PREDICTS, he forecast that in 1981 all newspapers, magazines, and books would be printed on spun plastic, and they would come from a slot in your wall which would be radio-controlled. In another prediction, he said that in the late 1970s, a woman physicist would develop a theory of magnetism that overcomes gravity. This discovery would result in aircraft and space vehicles that require no sustained rocketry propulsion. Let's not forget his prediction that by the year 1980, America would face a shortage of cemeteries. Construction would begin on the world's largest cemetery, large enough to accommodate ten million bodies with crypt facilities for fifty million more. It would be constructed in the state of Nevada.

In the 1960s, Criswell was often a guest on the Tonight Show hosted by Johnny Carson. Criswell would make these outlandish predictions while Johnny Carson made witty comments on each, causing the audience to laugh uproariously. No one took Criswell's prophecies seriously, and everyone enjoyed the bantering between Johnny, his sidekick Ed McMahon, and guest Criswell. If Criswell's predictions turned out to be accurate, he'd never set foot on the Tonight Show. The audience would have been fearful of the predictions he made, and no witty remarks would make the audience either in the studio or at home laugh.

Openly predicting or giving information attained through your paranormal talent, especially if you are known for your accuracy, will only lead to trouble. When I receive information that I think is life-threatening, I feel that I have a moral responsibility to pass that information onto those directly involved. They can use it or ignore it, yet I feel justified in alerting or warning them. This course of action has caused trouble for me. By giving bad news, the phrase, "Kill the messenger" comes into play. Many people seem to believe that if you deliver the message of an upcoming problem, you are responsible for causing it to happen. From that point on, they won't like you and will try to discredit you. Discrediting you and dismissing your cautions makes them feel safer. Their logic is that if I don't believe your warnings, it won't happen. On a more positive note, you may have saved someone's life or helped them to avert a catastrophe. My thought is that if I saved someone's life or diverted a disaster, then it was all worth it.

You can also be passive, tell no one what you see, and you will cause no ill feeling and can go on with your life. You won't be ridiculed. You can keep your information stored deep inside you. It's up to you. But think, if you get a message that someone will suffer harm and you keep that knowledge to yourself, can you live with the consequences?

Life's journey starts with birth and ends with death. How you navigate those in-between years is up to you. From 1902 to 1909, Albert Einstein worked at a Swiss patent office in Bern. He impressed his superiors with his handling and understanding of complicated technical patents and could have had a remarkable and rewarding career working there for the rest of his life. Einstein called his time there as his "worldly cloister" and, in his spare time, filed his own patents such as the electro-mechanical synchronization of time. Working in a patent office wasn't for him, and he ventured out from his safe place. He had his share of disbelievers and some of the experts of the time thought he was unbalanced, but he persevered doing what he believed was right. The rest is history, and he's known worldwide for his accomplishments.

Speaking for myself, I don't make my unusual abilities my mission in life; they're only a part of it. Since my early teen years, I've always had a job, and later I started a career in forensic videography and photography. I fix and service my cars and truck and do repairs around the house when needed. By doing this, I'm always keeping one foot in reality, which keeps my mind focused.

I don't fear the dead. For years I've managed to be somehow a conduit in communicating with them, that's if they choose to communicate with me. It doesn't always work as you would think. I'm far from Whoopie Goldberg's character, Oda Mae Brown, a Spiritual Advisor/Spiritual Reader in the film, Ghosts. When spirits communicate, I've found that they may use words or images, and it's left to me to determine what they are trying to say. They may enter my mind in my sleep or make themselves known right in the middle of the day while I'm washing my car.

This leads to the question, is there life after death? Without hesitation, my answer is yes. There is no way the information I gather from a person who has passed is something I could acquire from other means. Contrary to popular belief, a person like me cannot get intimate personal information about someone from the Internet. You can spend days on your computer with every search engine known to man, and you still wouldn't know what color my departed Aunt liked or what was the first car she bought in 1948.

So, what happens after death? Of course, the physical body is disposed of or interred; it's the inner self or soul that lives on. Some religions say it's taken to heaven or its interpretation of a perfect dwelling after death. In my opinion, the soul after death slips out of its corporeal frame and enters an alternate realm. The soul goes to a place one would consider to be a holding area where some reincarnate into another living body or remain in this place for an undetermined time. Some of these souls may watch over their earthly living family and occasionally make their presence known through odd feelings, dreams, or even a ghostly visitation. Stories tell of these spirits forewarning their earthbound friends and relatives of a pending tragedy, sent through visions that are much more pronounced than mere dreams.

Some souls left this earth with unresolved truths. A person who died could have been blamed falsely for wrongdoing. Those left behind perpetuate this falsehood of misinformation initially concocted by someone because of jealousy or even revenge. I'm sure it is cruel and unsettling for someone who crossed over knowing that for years, generations, or even eternity, their name will be linked to an uncomplimentary, fictional account of their life. This anguish has caused many a soul to take out its frustration through poltergeist[1] activity in someone's home.

Through all of this, where do we, "the odd ones," fit? Maybe we should consider that we are all born with various types of filters. For example, most of us have a filter that prevents us from seeing, hearing, or sensing many things. Dogs can smell a thousand times better than humans, some birds like an owl can see in almost total darkness, and my cat can hear sounds that the best microphone can't pick up. Compared to these animals, we are superior beings; we only lack some of their super capabilities. When I see an entity that others can't, it's probably due to my flawed or different filter, allowing me to see and hear what others can't.

When I investigate with someone like Psychic Paula Roberts, how strange it must look to an outsider to watch us walk through a building seeing and sensing something they can't. Yes, I'm aware it seems odd, but what we see and feel is real.

In Heaven, what do the souls do? I'd like to believe we possibly go back in time, reentering their bodies to relive our life all over again. This second chance would allow us to correct the mistakes we made the first time.

Now you have a good idea of where I'm coming from. Should people disbelieve the existence of paranormal abilities, that is something I can't change. I am not a missionary sent to convince others to believe in this.

Once I'm gone, I don't know what legacy or impact I'll leave behind. In time, maybe my views will be tested and proven right. Which brings us back to the afterlife. I see it as a place where the

---

[1] (pol-ter-geist) a noisy spirit.

discomfort of physical and emotional pain experienced during life is gone. It is a joyous place where time stands still. A place where souls enjoy the good times that life awarded them. This is why I'm convinced that somewhere the dead are singing,

*And sometimes I can hear them.*

Made in the USA
Middletown, DE
24 July 2021